NEVER
—HAVE A—
BAD DAY

A GUIDE TO A LIFESTYLE OF LEADERSHIP

Kelvin A. Waites, Sr.

Nasim Al-Hakim

Dr. Deshawn Rouse

ISBN-13: 978-1-7346860-2-9

ISBN-978-0-578-75440-6

DEDICATIONS

Kelvin A. Waites, Sr.

I dedicate this book to all leaders across this globe. This book was written as a tool for you to use as a reference as you continue your journey on the road of leadership. I hope that you can use this book as a lamp when things get dark to lighten up your pathway as you continue to lead your people. This book was written at one of the toughest times in my life. It was written during the Covid-19 virus that has taken many lives, as well as during a time in our country when there is an unprecedented outcry for civil justice. This book is so relevant to what is going on in our world today.

Dr. Deshawn Rouse

I would love to dedicate this book to my wife Debra and my handsome sons Tanique, Kenly, and Jordan. I would also like to dedicate this book in memory of my mother Ellen Rouse. and to my father Jacob Rouse.

TABLE OF CONTENTS

Acknowledgments

ACKNOWLEDGMENTS

Kelvin A. Waites, Sr.

First and foremost, I would like to thank God for ordering my steps in d leadership journey thus far. Also, I would like to thank my father, the late Isaac Waites Sr., for planting a seed in me that continues to still grow today. He was a master at motivating and inspiring, not so much with his words, but with the way he lived his life. If it were not for Isaac Waites Sr., I would not be the leader that I am today for my family, as well as for the people that I am charged with leading. He truly left a legacy that has no sign of fading away any time soon.

I would also like to thank my mother, Frances Waites, for always praying for me and encouraging me to keep pushing forward. She always reminds me that my father would tell me to "reach for the sky because the sky is the limit.

I thank my brothers Isaac Waites Jr and Terrance Waites for being the men that our father raised us to be. I appreciate the two of you always being there, even though we all live many miles apart. I am certain that the relationship that we have causes our father to smile in heaven.

I would like to thank my friends and colleagues who have helped me to grow over the years. I have been encouraged, motivated, and inspired by many of you.

Finally, I would like to thank my wife Chelice Waites, my daughter Jasmin Waites, and my son Kelvin Waites Jr., for standing by my side while I served for several years in the United States Army, as well as law enforcement. I know that it has not always been a walk in the park. I could not have done this without you.

Nasim Al-Hakim, CMB

The completion of this project could not have been possible without the assistance and support of my family and friends throughout my life. All your names may not be enumerated. However, your contributions are sincerely appreciated, and I am grateful for having you in my life.

I want to dedicate this book to two people that have made a huge impact in my life. Special thanks to my niece, Caliyah Marlei Ross for blessing me with the responsibility of being your uncle and leader. You are the reason that I push myself every day to be the best that I can be. Your bravery, confidence, and determination are second to none. I am so proud of you.

Finally, this book is dedicated to loving the memory of my brother and friend, Luit Woodberry. Words cannot express the infinite wisdom and knowledge that you have shared with me and so many others during your time here. Rest assured, you will always be remembered and loved. Rest well, my Brother.

CHAPTER 1

THE FOUNDATION OF LEADERSHIP

Leadership nuggets covered in this chapter:

- ❖ Establishing a foundation for leadership.

- ❖ How a leader's foundation will support their leadership model.

- ❖ The impact of constant updates on a leader's progress.

Kelvin A. Waites, Sr.

The foundation of leadership begins with and is built on integrity. It does not matter how much education and experience you have. If you do not have integrity, then the foundation of your leadership will be suspect to anything that could destroy it. Therefore, your leadership must start and end with integrity.

Integrity is having the willpower to do the right thing all the time, even when it does not feel good or is not the most popular decision.

A leader that served on my team once asked me, "Chief, how do you manage to make decisions that impact the lives of people without cracking or folding under pressure?"

He went on to say, "I see you do it daily, time after time, without batting an eye."

I told him that I can sleep at night because I do my best to use integrity with every decision that I make.

When I talk about integrity, I am referring to the principle behind how a leader hires, disciplines, and promotes within their companies or organizations. This also includes the way a leader handles employee, citizen, and customer complaints.

I am committed to doing what is in the best interest of the organization, not what is in the best interest of the workplace cliques or an individual. When your focus is on doing what is in the best interest of the organization, every single time, everything else will fall into place.

> The foundation of the leadership model
> is important...it is designed to hold the
> weight of the structure.

Kelvin A. Waites, Sr.

As leaders, we must promote an atmosphere where we look at every concern individually and objectively, so that if something is broken, we can address it appropriately and fix it. At the end of the day, it is all about getting better and getting to the next level. So many times, people take the word integrity for granted. As a result, it becomes a cliché that leaders love to throw around. However, the integrity of a structure can be a matter of life or death.

Webster's Dictionary defines integrity as "an unimpaired condition, soundness or the quality or state of being complete or undivided." I had a good friend tell me once that "the people that you are called to lead don't necessarily expect you to be tough, but they do expect you to make tough decisions." When your leadership is built on the foundation of integrity, many of your decisions will be tough.

The foundation of a leader's leadership model is important because, just like the foundation of a building, it is designed to hold the weight of the structure. The leader's leadership model acts as an anchor for the structure and protects the foundation from moisture or other outside influences that could break it down.

Most leaders will acknowledge that the strength of any structure is found within its foundation. Therefore, a leader's leadership model sets the tone for everything. No structure can hold up to the elements and stand the test of time without a solid foundation. We must lay our foundation and then build from there.

Since the foundation holds the entire structure up, if it is not put together well, it can succumb to the elements of the environment it is in. The water will wash it away, the wind will blow it down, and your structure will fail.

We have all heard that phrase "if you don't stand for something, you will fall for anything". I believe this is true of a leader's leadership model. If something were to happen and you were no longer there for your people, you would want the leadership foundation that you built to hold, right?

Right!

You would not want all the progress that your organization has made to fall by the wayside just because you were no longer in place or you were not there physically.

When your leadership is built on the foundation of integrity, many of your decisions will be tough.

Kelvin A. Waites, Sr.

Constant updates are also important to a leader's progress because leaders must stay relevant and up to speed on what is going on. If you are going to be a great leader, you must be a lifelong learner. Policies, procedures, and best practices change daily. Leaders should either aggressively continue to seek the newest advancements in their profession or, have someone dedicated to their teams or staff who search for these advancements relentlessly.

We should all be looking for ways to work smarter and not harder. Once we, as leaders, start to believe that we have it all figured out, we are setting ourselves up for failure.

Things change around us all the time and we must keep up. We cannot let our leadership get stale because if we do, we will lose the people that we are called to lead. When I refer to a leader's leadership getting stale, I mean that they are stuck in the rut of doing it how they have always done it because it is comfortable. Somebody once said that "if we're standing still then we are falling behind" and we cannot afford to fall behind in this ever-changing, fast-paced world.

Leaders must continuously stretch themselves and grow. The only way to do that is to continue to study, learn, and reinvent ourselves repeatedly. Not only should we continue to learn, but we should encourage our people to do the same.

Nasim Al-Hakim, CMB

The foundation of leadership should be deeply rooted in passion. The keys to having a strong foundation in leadership are commitment, humility, resilience, empathy, persistence, self-awareness, vision, and a willingness to work on personal development. Passion is paramount to a leader's success because it is the key driver of enthusiasm and a leader's desire to achieve their goals.

> The foundation of leadership should be
> deeply rooted in passion.
>
> *Nasim Al-Hakim, CMB*

Life experiences play a big part in a leader's foundation as well. A leader could possess all the passion, all the commitment, and willingness to work, but if they have not been through adversity, then it is hard to quantify your leadership. I believe that leadership is tested on the battlefield and measured by your growth thereafter.

Your foundation will remind you of your "why" when you hit tough times in leadership. Everyone has a "why", right? Everyone has a reason behind what they do or something that keeps them waking up every morning ready to conquer the day ahead.

What is your "why"?

For a lot of people, it is their children, their family, their personal growth, or even negative experiences that propel them to do better. There is a lot that can go into your "why", and the foundation I mentioned earlier is directly impacted by your why.

Your "why" can be contagious. When others see how

A big part of leadership and having self-awareness is having the ability to meet people where they are.

Nasim Al-Hakim, CMB

strongly you are committed to your purpose, it helps them to find their "why" as well. As you work to satisfy your" why", you can unknowingly provide a path for others to travel as they fulfill their "why".

A playbook is also vital to the quality of a leader's foundation. A playbook consists of strategic planning, goals, shared vision, operating procedures, and cultural values. This playbook gives the leader the ability to adjust sails as needed without losing sight of what is important. It also allows the leader to serve in more areas and aspects of leadership. Simply put, it expands your reach as a leader and provides the tools needed to achieve goals and be successful.

As we mature and move higher in leadership, many times we get disconnected from the people we are called to lead. Leaders need to be intentional about connecting and seeing things through the eyes of others. If any leader fails to do this, they will find it nearly impossible to communicate effectively and connect with the team of people they are called to lead.

A big part of leadership and self-awareness is having the ability to meet people where they are. If you are not meeting people where they are, you are not going to be able to change the climate or lift them.

Constant updates are important because they allow you to connect with others, reset expectations, and provide a new path moving forward. Remember, communication is key but connecting is of utmost. There is a distinct difference between the two.

Dr. Deshawn Rouse

The foundation of leadership should consist of these three components: wisdom, humility, and tenacity.

Every leader should possess wisdom. Since I am a pastor, I always refer to the Bible for direction in the area of leadership and there is a story of a King named Solomon, who once prayed, "Lord teach me how to deal with your people" (I Kings 3:9-11 NIV).

The Lord responds to King Solomon's prayer by granting him the wisdom that he needed to deal with the people. Wisdom is a must in the foundation of every leader.

Humility is another essential component of the leadership foundation. Finding a way to serve those that serve you is what it means to be humble. You must be willing to serve others over yourself and show people that you care by being passionate about them and their needs. I see myself as a servant leader, not the one in the front of the room, but the leader providing support in the back of the room.

The last thing that every leadership foundation should have is tenacity. You must be strong. You must be resilient. You must show people that you will not give up under pressure and that you are willing to be in it for the long haul. Even when things do not look like they are lining up, you must have tenacity.

These three things, wisdom, humility, and tenacity should be a part of every leader's foundation because they help to put that leader on a trajectory bound for success. If you have them as a part of your leadership foundation, then you will lead your company, business, family, and/or organization with excellence. But if you are a leader who eliminates these principles from your leadership foundation, you will be vulnerable to doing or saying anything.

Every decision you make will be based upon having wisdom, having humility, and having tenacity. I believe when a leader knows what their foundational models are, they will be able to use them in everyday life experiences. Your foundational model should be set before adventuring into anything.

The foundation of leadership should
consist of these three components:
wisdom, humility, and tenacity.

Dr. Deshawn Rouse

In addition to the foundation, I think constant updates are important to a leader's progress. Just like modern technology such as iPhones® and Apple iPads®, leaders are constantly being sent updates. It is up to the individual to accept the updates or not. But if we do accept them, we will find that our device runs more efficiently, and we will have access to the latest technological advances.

On the other hand, if someone refuses to accept the updates, they find themselves leading and making decisions from outdated information.

I have seen a lot of leaders in the church world who still have a point of view from the 1970s and 1980s, even though they are dealing with the millennial church. This has caused them to become frustrated because what used to work for them no longer works today.

You must be willing to get updates through training so you can find out if what you are doing will serve your organization today. This is true of your marriage or any other relationship in your life, if you want it to thrive, you must accept the updates.

Sometimes updates take a while. It may take a few minutes, a few hours, or overnight before the updates are done, but you must be willing to go through the process of removing outdated information from your leadership style.

Taking this into consideration, a leading tech once asked its users why they do not update their computers. Two of the four responses given are the same reasons I think many leaders choose not to update their leadership styles. The first response was that they were uninformed about the benefits of the updates and the second one was that they were comfortable with their current setup.

> Just like modern technology… we are constantly being sent updates as leaders.

Dr. Deshawn Rouse

Just like those software users, many leaders will find that the old way no longer produces results. Their teams will stop responding and progression will come to a halt. If a leader is going to remain relevant, bring about any growth, or maintain a "virus-free" environment for their teams, then constant updates of their leadership styles will be a necessity.

CHAPTER 2

LEADERS ARE BORN OR MADE

Leadership nuggets covered in this chapter:

❖ Leaders are born or made.

❖ Life provides opportunities to grow as a leader.

❖ The importance of being grounded in mind, body, and spirit.

Kelvin A. Waites, Sr.

I am sure you have heard the question "are leaders born or made?" I do not think it is one or the other, but both. In my case, I think I am a "made" leader, who was mentored and taught to lead by a father, who had no idea what kind of seeds he was planting in me.

Let me explain.

When I was a little boy, I never displayed any leadership qualities that stood out to me and I did not have any aspirations to lead others. My father, Isaac Waites Sr., was the greatest leader that I have ever known, but the leadership did not manifest itself in me right away.

On many occasions, under not-so-ideal circumstances, I watched my father take care of our family. He thrived under pressure and even when the path did not seem to be clear, he had a quiet confidence that just could not be denied. He made it easy for everyone around him to follow his lead. The time during my childhood would prove to be crucial in making me a leader.

I never really fit in with any of the other kids because I was born with crooked legs and wore leg braces just like Forrest Gump did in the movie. I also suffered from chronic and severe asthma. The slightest dust particles that I encountered would cause me to have a violent asthma attack and I would have to be treated with a shot at the local emergency room. During this time in my youth, I lacked confidence and I did not even believe that my life would amount to anything. I could not lead myself, therefore, I did not have anyone willing to follow me.

Back then, the highlight of most of my days was when the elevator in my building was working so my older brother and I would not have to walk up fourteen flights of stairs to get home.

We lived on the 14th floor of the projects in Harlem, New York, and walking those stairs was hard for me because of those crooked legs and asthma I was challenged with. Many days I suffered an asthma attack right there in the stairwell. Other times, I had to stop and rest because of the pain in my legs.

When the elevator did work, most times it would only go half the way up. Then my older brother and I would have to climb out in between floors and still walk the stairs. Thinking back, I realize how crazy it was for us to climb out of the elevator without knowing if it would start up again and cut us in half.

I know my childhood challenges sound rough, but those experiences taught me many valuable lessons that still serve me today.

One of those lessons is that there will not be any magical elevators that will come along and carry me to any level of success, I will have to walk up the stairs, no matter what.

I survived growing up in Harlem until one day my parents decided that the city was too rough to try to raise two small boys. They sacrificed, saved up money, and moved our family to Charleston, South Carolina. This is when my asthma started to clear up and those Forrest Gump leg braces had my legs as straight as they would ever get.

This was the first time in my life that I was able to go outside and play as normal kids did. I overcame my challenges with asthma and crooked legs and began to excel in football and basketball. This is when I noticed other kids following my lead.

Keeping my composure, never complaining about anything, and always giving 110% effort were leadership traits molded in me by my father and they began to stand out as I played organized sports. These same traits have made me the great leader I am today.

Merely possessing these leadership qualities did not put me into the position of leadership right off. For many years, it seemed like I was being hidden in the shadows, learning, and training for the appropriate time to step into a leadership role. It was through these opportunities in life that I was "drafted" into the role of a leader.

My first meaningful role in leadership came when I served as a squad leader in the United States Army during basic training at Fort Jackson in Columbia, South Carolina. This role was crucial in my development as a leader. Then my dad, the molder of my leadership style, died and the leadership traits I learned from him were being tested through adversity.

Being asked to speak at my father's funeral as a representative for our family was one of the hardest things I have ever had to do. This is when I learned that the hard things we do as leaders will always stretch us and help us grow into better leaders.

One of those lessons... there are no magical elevators that will come along and carry me to any level of success. I must walk up the stairs, no matter what.

Kelvin A. Waites, Sr.

When I was hired as a Captain at a local law enforcement organization, I was an outsider and once again found myself relying heavily on those traits I learned from my father. I was joining a new organization at the executive level and the red carpet was not rolled out for my arrival. It was a challenging experience, but it proved to be a gift that prepared me for my next steps in leadership.

My next opportunity for growth in my career came when I was appointed to be the Deputy Chief of Police for one of the largest counties in the state of South Carolina. During my time there, I found myself thrust into the role of Interim Chief of Police. Talk about stretching and growing. I felt like a 16-year-old basketball player who grew a foot and a half over the summer. I had to go out and get new clothes that fit me if you know what I mean. Not even realizing it, that experience was preparing me for my current leadership role as Chief of Police.

Those were some great growth opportunities, but my greatest opportunity came 26 years ago on March 19, 1994, when I married my wife and we started a family. Soon after getting married, my wife and I received orders from the United States Army to go to Augsburg, Germany.

Living in a foreign country while raising our daughter and son with nobody to depend on except God and each other certainly stretched me outside of my comfort zone. This is when I developed my vision as a leader. I was able to see what my father saw when he guided our family when I was a child. I would lean on some of those lessons I learned in my childhood as I guided my own family.

This experience and opportunity to grow as a husband and father have been my greatest tests and my greatest achievements. Both of my children are college graduates and as I write this book, my daughter is attending law school.

My father, the greatest leader that I have ever known, only had a 6th-grade education and my mom never finished high school, but I know that I have made them proud by continuing the legacy of leadership and excellence they molded into me and my brothers.

Life has afforded me many opportunities to grow as a leader for which I am thankful, humbled, and blessed. I still wake up every single day excited about the opportunity to lead, but even more excited about the opportunity to continue to grow and learn as it relates to this marathon that we are all running as leaders.

Every leader should embrace and cherish their opportunities to lead because it is a privilege and a blessing to lead people.

As a leader grows, they need to maintain balance in their life. I did not always do this, but as I stretched and grew, I learned to do like some NFL quarterbacks have done over time. I learned how to let the game slow down for me. I would tune in to the game plan and the mission, rehearse and practice until my muscle memory kicked in, and everything appeared to be moving in slow motion.

When we are grounded as it relates to our minds, bodies, and spirits, we can lead at a high level and it seems as if everything is in slow motion.

You have all heard the phrase "too much of anything

is not good for you." If you have too much going on in your mind, then you will not be prepared to handle the daily decisions and multiple situations that you will face as a leader.

As it relates to mental health, leaders sometimes believe they are superheroes and can do it all by themselves. This attitude is dangerous to our success as well as the success of our teams and organizations. No one can do it alone, so do not let your pride get in the way of your healing and having a breakthrough. If you find yourself struggling or feeling stuck, get help.

Leaders must also keep their bodies conditioned to be able to deal with the stress and pressure that goes

---

Every leader should embrace and
cherish the opportunity to lead,
because it is a privilege and a blessing
to lead people.

Kelvin A. Waites, Sr.

along with leading. Our bodies all react differently when we are under stress and pressure, whether we realize it or not. Taking a brisk walk, making physical fitness a way of life, or even doing controlled breathing techniques daily can have a major and positive impact on you as a leader.

Scheduling regular doctor's visits is another way a

leader can take care of themselves. Do not wait until you break down completely to get fixed. Just like preventive maintenance increases the life expectancy of a vehicle, it will do the same for us as leaders, if we take preventive maintenance seriously.

Our spirit is who we are and what we believe in. Things will happen to make us question our faith, destiny, and even our hope. We must guard our spirituality like Fort Knox and keep it grounded by walking in the path that we believe God has destined for us to walk in.

Take time for yourself to reflect, meditate, and recharge. Remember, that if we are not the absolute best version of ourselves, then we are indirectly cheating the people we are called to lead out of the highest level of leadership they should be receiving from us.

Nasim Al-Hakim, CMB

I believe leaders are a combination of being both, born and made.

Early on in life, I exhibited a gift of leadership. I was never a follower but was always very independent and confident in myself. Through experience, I have grown into a better leader and I have been able to harness my vision as a leader. I have learned how to structure my path, my thoughts, my innate qualities, and my life experiences in a way that becomes fuel for my journey and equips me to lead others. It is this combination of being born and made, that I accredit my effectiveness as a leader.

> Life will afford you many
> opportunities, but it is what you do
> with those opportunities that help you
> grow as a leader.

Nasim Al-Hakim, CMB

Life will afford you many opportunities, but it is what you do with those opportunities that help you grow as a leader. At times, one could argue what came first: the chicken or the egg? This is true as it relates to opportunities and growth. Opportunities exist, but if one does not take advantage of them, or understand what the journey is about, I do not believe that he or she will grow.

First, it is identifying what those opportunities are, and second, deciding what you are going to do with them to execute. That is especially important because, at the end of the day, the opportunity exists daily, but everyone is not traveling to the same destination in life. Often you will be on the road less traveled without a blueprint or map and must remain vigilant.

Being grounded and having the self-awareness to learn who you are, understand your core values and your beliefs is important to forming your foundation.

Nasim Al-Hakim, CMB

Being grounded and having the self-awareness to learn who you are, understand your core values and your beliefs is important to forming your foundation. This helps you to remain focused and keeps you aligned with your purpose through difficult or uncertain times.

The ability to be flexible or fluid as you grow and expand your foundation is important. So often we are stuck in the leadership of the past and not open to change. In my eyes, I am not changing my foundation of leadership. Thus, adding some additional key ingredients that are needed for me to be more effective.

Dr. Deshawn Rouse

An immensely powerful question to ask any leader is "are you a born leader or a made leader?" As I ponder this question regarding my leadership, I believe it is both. God has placed in all of us certain leadership qualities that He gave to us because of who we are and our unique assignment on this Earth. God will then place you in situations around other people that will help to sharpen those leadership abilities that lie within you.

Be mindful... you do not want to make the mistake of running away from the person who has been assigned to sharpen the leadership gift inside of you.

Dr. Deshawn Rouse

In the Bible, there is a scripture that says, "As iron sharpens iron, so does one man another" (Proverbs 27:17 NIV). I believe that even though you may be a leader, you can always use sharpening from other leaders so you can be more effective in the area that God has called you to. No matter the task, make sure you are like a sharp ax and not a dull one. A dull ax will take longer to get something done, but a sharp ax will get it done more quickly and efficiently because it has allowed itself to be sharpened by other ax files (leaders).

United States President Abraham Lincoln said, "Give me six hours to chop down a tree and I will spend the first four sharpening the ax." I believe that God is making you by placing you around certain leaders who will constantly sharpen you. These people may sometimes rub you the wrong way, but their job is to rub away the dullness to reveal your sharpness. Be mindful of this the next time you find yourself in a difficult experience with someone, you do not want to make the mistake of running away from the person who has been assigned to sharpen the leadership gift inside of you.

My life has provided me with the opportunity to be a pastor and I believe that this has helped me over the years as a leader. I have been pastoring for 21 years, but when I started, I was a novice pastor with a young congregation. Back then, I pastored people based on how I saw other seasoned pastors lead their congregations. Many of those congregations were older and conservative, but my members were a millennial church, younger and more progressive.

During these years of pastoring, my congregation has taught me how to be a pastor to them. I have had to tailor my leadership to the times we live in today by embracing the unique abilities of the millennial church, understanding what they bring to the table, and connecting with them from where they are. My church has allowed me the beautiful experience to develop as a strong leader by enabling me to stay in touch with the past while relating to the future.

In addition to taking time off, leaders must incorporate regular exercise into their lifestyle.

Dr. Deshawn Rouse

It is particularly important for leaders to be grounded as it relates to their mind, body, and spirit because the very task of being a leader is so demanding. You need to have all three of these areas aligned. I think every leader should be able to take care of their mental health by taking time off for themselves. This allows them to push the reset button and they can come back before their people, family, friends, and/or business and not be exhausted. In addition to taking time off, leaders need to incorporate regular exercise into their lifestyles. This helps to keep their bodies functioning properly. It has been proven that exercising helps the mind think more clearly.

Finally, I believe that everyone needs to have that time that they need to get in touch with their creator, God, who made them and knows how to re-center them back to their true purpose and mission. Many leaders operate and they are burnt out and it affects their bodies, homes, and workplace.

CHAPTER 3

THE LOOK OF LEADERSHIP

Leadership nuggets covered in this chapter:

❖ What leadership looks like.

❖ Animals that symbolize leadership and why.

❖ How your leadership looks to those you lead.

Kelvin A. Waites, Sr.

Leadership looks different to everyone. I see a display of leadership as a group of people, working together with a common cause, with a leader so embedded within the group that you cannot even tell who the leader is. I am also inspired by those leaders who can influence others around them without barking out orders or telling people what to do, but simply by their actions.

Tom Landry, who was the great Hall of Fame Dallas Cowboys football coach, once said that "leadership is getting people to do what they don't want to do to achieve what they want to achieve."

Compassion and a commitment to serving the people you are tasked with leading is another look of leadership. Some may wonder, "how can you lead and serve at the same time?"

You serve your people by making sure they have everything that they need to do their jobs effectively and efficiently. When you build and lift your people instead of tearing them down, you are serving them.

Having compassion for the personal and professional needs of your team should be the number one priority of any leader. If you are always dictating your demands, never getting feedback, or allowing your team to have a voice, then you will be a disconnected leader.

People want to know that you care and when they believe that you do, they will buy into your mission.

There are times when leadership will look dark in terms of what pathway a team, a family, a group, or an organization needs to go. But the leader must find a way to lead the group through the darkness to the light.

It may not be through policies, procedures, cheat sheets or some type of hidden treasure map. Instead, it will be through fortitude, courage, and gumption to know that if you just push and pull the group forward, the storm will pass, and the path will once again be clear.

You serve your people by making sure they have everything that they need to do their jobs effectively and efficiently.

Kelvin A. Waites, Sr.

Every leader will experience times when everyone will not be on board with their plans or decisions. At times like this, a leader must stand firm and believe in the effectiveness of their leadership. Even if you must drag people, the leader's job is to get the team to the finish line. Remember, great leaders, are respected but not always liked by all.

My zodiac sign is Leo and when I consider leadership, the term "king of the jungle" often comes to mind. In every walk of life, the figure of a lion represents power, tenacity, and courage.

Another animal I relate to leadership is the eagle. I view the eagle as a leader that makes sure their people have what they need to flourish and complete their mission without micromanaging how it gets done.

Just like an eagle, I can hover nearby my team, observing what goes on without getting fully involved and overbearing. I allow my team to spread their wings by empowering them to figure things out on their own. However, I do remain in proximity just in case I need to swoop down to any level and resolve issues that may arise.

Eagles are also a great reminder that leaders must have the ability to rise above the gossip, the rumors, the negativity, and the drama if they are going to succeed at focusing on the mission at hand.

Leaders should have some idea of how others see their leadership. Not because they are trying to be liked by people, but because they recognize that without people, they will not be a leader.

Knowing how others see your leadership provides an understanding of the impact you are having on others and how effective you have been. It also allows you to take self-inventory of what is or is not working in your leadership style so you can adjust if needed.

My team would probably describe me as a passionate leader who is always fired up and excited about serving them. I would agree with that assessment and I expect them to match my intensity. I am dedicated to leading and pushing the people within my organization to reach their full potential. If I do not get the effort needed to reach the level of excellence that is expected from them, I have no problem addressing it. One of my favorite sayings is "don't just be good, be good for something" and this is something I live by.

> One of my favorite sayings is "don't just
> be good, be good for something" and
> this is something I live by.
>
> *Kelvin A. Waites, Sr.*

I provide my team with a positive work environment where everyone's creativity is welcomed and nourished. They will tell you that I have their backs and would do anything that I can do to help them. On the flip side, they would also tell you that if there are issues, challenges, or concerns, I bring them to the forefront so that we can address them.

People in my community would tell me that I work hard to make everyone in the room feel important.

They would say that when I am involved in a project, I am in and that I make everyone else around me better. I am known as the ultimate team player, always acknowledging that none of us can get it done on our own.

When it comes to my family, they will tell you that I have embraced my leadership role within the family, and I take it very seriously. They would say that I am loving, caring and that I push them all to be the absolute best that they can be. Sometimes I am so positive that it gets on their nerves. They call me "Mr. Calm" and my wife says, "you never get rattled."

Ultimately, my team, my community, and my family would say the same thing, "through the good, the bad, and the ugly, they know that I will always have their backs".

Have you ever asked others how they see you as a leader?

I encourage you to do so. The words of those that you lead can be just what the doctor ordered when you are wounded. It just might surprise you to find out that you are having more of an impact than you expected.

Nasim Al-Hakim, CMB

When it comes to the look of leadership, I believe it has more to do with an individual's behavior than it does with their outward appearance. In a leader's daily workings, their behavior will always be on display and those they lead will be directly or indirectly impacted by that behavior. Therefore, a leader must always be mindful of their behavior and the message it sends to those around them.

There are three behavioral characteristics that I believe make a good leader a great leader. They are energy, enthusiasm, and execution. When I think of energy, I think about wellness, mental, physical, social, and emotional wellness. Energy is needed to sustain your enthusiasm as you move forward to fulling your daily goals.

> Within all species of animals, there is a
> leader who leads them.

Nasim Al-Hakim, CMB

Enthusiasm is extremely important. It is the key driver of passion. Enthusiasm means having an active and motivated attitude toward a goal. Finally, execution is carrying out or putting into effect a plan, order, or course of action. Energy, enthusiasm, and execution, in that order, are key for a leader to exhibit.

Leadership is balancing the responsibility for others while caring for your dreams and journey. It is not a destination to arrive at, so to speak, but it is a continuous journey of life and growth. This journey is ever-evolving, changing, fluid, and organic.

Many people use animals to symbolize leadership. It is tough for me to narrow it down to just one animal because there are several animals, within their species, that I relate to leadership.

If you are talking about an aspect of being a hawk or a bird, you talk about the freedom to fly about and soar. Birds also represent reaching new heights, levels, and having more geographical range than other animals.

If you consider the elephant, one of the largest animals on land, you will talk about their memory and size, and sociability. But do not be fooled, if pushed, elephants will let you know what they can do to protect themselves.

The lion is another animal that many relate to leadership because of its dominance and strength. But then again, you could talk about the hyenas and how they come together in packs. So, I truly do not believe that there is one specific animal that exhibits what leadership looks like. Within all species of animals, there is a leader who leads them. This is a great example of diversity in leadership.

My team and others that I serve would probably describe me as an inspirational leader that is knowledgeable, that motivates, coaches, supports and encourages them. I would have to agree because I have high expectations for myself as a leader; I always strive to be competent, responsive, reliable, and empathetic to them and their needs.

I think of myself as a fanatic when it comes to my team. Now, you may be thinking of a fanatic negatively, but I think of it a little differently.

This is one key thing about leadership, you must be a fanatic for others to really see or feel how contagious it can be for ourselves.

Nasim Al-Hakim, CMB

When I hear the word fanatic, I think of the person that has their shirt off, their chest and face painted, all while attending a football game in Green Bay, Wisconsin when it is 10 below zero. They are going wild in support of their team, while others are looking at them as if they are insane.

This fan is never distracted by the thoughts of what they may look like to those around. Instead only focused on energizing their team to play harder and win. Teams look for this kind of fan, especially when times get tough on the field. The team might even say to themselves, "If I do not play for anybody else, I am going to do it for that one fanatic fan".

I am that fanatic for my team. I am the leader that will walk the walk with you until you get to the win. This is one key thing about leadership: you must be a fanatic for others to see or feel how contagious it can be. That explosive energy alone can ignite a team or a stadium.

Dr. Deshawn Rouse

According to Webster's dictionary, the character is defined as the mental and moral qualities distinctive to an individual. When I discuss what leadership looks like, I focus on the character of a leader. To take it a step further, the stability and consistency of that leader's character are what I look at.

A great example of this would be the keyboard.

Yes, a keyboard. It does not matter what device you are using, a computer, a phone, or touchscreen, the location of the characters on that keyboard are the same.

No matter the situation or circumstance, others come to depend on the leader who is stable in all their ways.

Dr. Deshawn Rouse

Stability and consistency are the elements that contribute to keyboard users being trained to type by feeling the location of the characters. Once trained, keyboard users are confident in their abilities and depend on the characters being in their place, no matter what keyboard they are using.

In the same way, a leader will gain the confidence of

those they are leading when their character is consistent. No matter the situation or circumstance, others come to depend on a leader who is stable in all their ways. When people can depend on a leader's character, they have a set example to go by and can grow successfully.

One of the worst things to see is a leader whose character is always changing. As leaders, we must make sure that we show our people what persistent character looks like by leading from a set of principles that allow us to control our emotions no matter the environment.

A lion is an animal that displays a great example of leadership. This is because a lion is persistent in pursuit of its prey. It moves slow and steady, taking as much time as needed to study the movements of its prey. When they strike, they will not miss. Sometimes, lions will sit for hours and scope out the weakest one. There is a famous quote that I heard about a lion and it is: "I will win, not immediately, but definitely."

If leadership were an animal, it would be a lion because all leaders must be resilient and willing to stay in it for the long haul. Take for instance, when I started my church in 1999, we began in my friend's living room. We had several people leave their places of fellowship to join ours. I know how that looked to some of their families and friends to hear that they left their churches to fellowship with a new ministry. One that does not even have a building. So, I began to tell them, "I will make sure we build a church for you all". It was tough in the beginning, but I remained persistent through the ups and downs. Within three short years, we built a church. Every leader must have the ability to say it and then do it.

No matter the situation or circumstance, others come to depend on the leader that is stable in all their ways.

Dr. Deshawn Rouse

I think my people would say I am consistent, persistent, and believe in structure and order. My people would say that I am like an astronomist, who looks at the big picture and the overall vision, to know where I am going. I am also like a microbiologist because I see the small details. An example of this would be when I knew how important it was to see the big picture of building a sanctuary and the details of checks and balances, budgeting, and being fiscally savvy.

People have also said that I am a very humble person and I like to serve people, which I believe are the major components needed to be an effective leader. The past 21 years have taught me not to just speak big but to plan big.

CHAPTER 4

NO LEADER IS PERFECT

Leadership nuggets covered in this chapter:

❖ Identifying character flaws and how to lead with a character flaw.

❖ How a leader bounces back from a bad decision.

❖ How leadership styles are developed.

Kelvin Waites

Every single leader has character flaws because nobody is perfect. Having a character flaw and being able to work around it calls for you, as a leader, to have the ability to be transparent with yourself. As leaders, we can mislead people all we want, but if we are going to be successful in leadership, we must make certain that we are truthful with ourselves.

My character flaw has always been the fact that I am skeptical and suspicious of everyone until I see that people have a genuine and sincere agenda. Most people trust people until they have a reason not to, but I am wired differently and will not trust anyone until they give me a reason to.

To improve and address this character flaw, I have conditioned myself to make intentional attempts at giving people the benefit of the doubt. A skill that I have mastered by setting this intention has been giving people an opportunity to earn my trust through menial interaction and tasks.

Being transparent with ourselves about who we are and what our character flaws are will allow us to build momentum while connecting and forming new relationships. Like this chapter's title so eloquently states, no leader is perfect.

As leaders, we can mislead people all
we want, but if we are going to be
successful in leadership, we must make
certain that we are truthful with
ourselves.

Kelvin A. Waites, Sr.

As leaders, we have staff and teams that work closely with us every day. We solicit feedback from them to assist us in making decisions knowing that at the end of the day, no matter what kind of feedback we get we will make the final decision.

But what do we do when we make bad decisions?

We cannot afford to blow it off like it is no big deal or act like it did not happen. If you do, you will lose credibility with your people.

It does not matter if we are responding in a public forum or dealing with our leadership team in-house, we must take full responsibility for our bad decisions.

Leaders set the tone, therefore, if we want to hold our teams accountable for the mistakes that they make, we must lead by example and hold ourselves accountable, first.

Acknowledging our mistakes, owning them, and learning from them is the kind of transparent accountability our teams will respect. It will make you, your team, and your organization better.

On the other hand, when the team wins, we need to

make certain that everyone understands that it is a total team effort. As leaders, we own the losses and find a way to get better from them, but we share the credit for victories with our team. It may seem hard, but it is fair when it comes to leadership.

A leadership style cannot be categorized into one size or one style that fits all. Our unique backgrounds, life experiences, beliefs, and values are what form our various leadership styles.

Because of my strong spiritual values, I would describe myself as a servant leader who brings about transformation in the lives of those that I lead. I believe that it is my job to serve my people by supporting them and giving them what they need to succeed.

Giving them what they need is not limited to work-related resources, it also entails having empathy for their personal needs.

 I work extremely hard to serve my people every opportunity that I get because I know the type of service that I expect them to render to the public. If my people never experience what it feels like to truly be served, then I cannot expect them to go out and serve our customers and the public the way that they deserve to be served.

My parents taught me that charity begins at home. Therefore, before I can serve the public, I must take care of my team first.

In addition to being a servant leader, I would also

As leaders, we own the losses and find
a way to get better from them, but we
share the credit for the victories with
our team.

Kelvin A. Waites, Sr.

describe myself as a transformational leader. I genuinely believe that part of my responsibility is to push everyone around me to step up their game while raising my level of play. I always try to come up with creative and out-of-the-box ways of doing things, while collecting agency-wide feedback from my people.

As a transformational leader, I continue to learn newer and more modern ways of doing things so I can keep my team moving forward. If there are changes that need to be made, I am willing to adjust where needed so we can keep up with the fast changes in society.

Nasim Al-Hakim, CMB

When I think about a character flaw, I think about it in terms of a person's strength. I envision a character flaw as overcompensating for one's strength.

For example, if you are a commander or leader of troops and you become overbearing, then it feels like you are abusing your authority and others find it hard to work in that environment.

In previous self-assessments in my life, I have learned that my five core strengths are individualization, self-awareness, being commander, focus, and being a realtor. Putting myself in the shoes of those I lead and examining how I use those strengths keeps me from overcompensating for them. That way my character flaws are not showing up in my leadership style.

> I envision a character flaw as
> overcompensating for one's strength.
>
> *Nasim Al-Hakim, CMB*

Character flaws should not be looked at as negative traits but as quality traits that need to be harnessed. The only thing I can relate this to is when parents are raising their children.

Being an overprotective parent appears as a character flaw, but it is a parent who loves and wants to protect their child a little more than what is deemed normal.

I do not see anything wrong with that.

I just think, as parents, we must learn that we are protecting them by delegating tasks to them and trusting they will be equipped to take on all challenges presented. When we allow our children to learn on their own, whatever that looks like, we now have balance and are maximizing our strength.

Character flaws should not be looked at
as negative traits but as quality traits
that need to be harnessed.

Nasim Al-Hakim, CMB

Leaders can bounce back from bad decisions by owning up to them, learning from them, and making the necessary corrections. Leadership is not about making the right call all the time, every day, or every second, but it is about the ability to make a call, period. If you remember to adjust your sails, correct if you are off course, and allow others to assist you in navigating, then you will get back on course.

My leadership style was developed from my experiences in life. I have always loved people and wanted to assist and help people. This desire is why servitude is embedded in my leadership style.

As I have grown in leadership, finance, as a sibling, being a friend, and an uncle, it has helped me to become more of a transformational and situational leader. These various roles have provided me with the tools needed to continue developing my skillset from a non-linear perspective. Thus, your leadership is not only defined by your success in the workplace.

Another aspect of my leadership style would be a strategy. Strategic leadership and planning are particularly important as you lead your process. It is important because it provides you with a blueprint, vision, and a plan to carry out your objectives along with a timeline to execute. I have learned to also adapt and adopt new areas slowly, as I grow and lead more people on my journey.

Dr. Deshawn Rouse

A character flaw that I have is being an introvert. If I do not have to talk, I will not and if I do not have to get up in front of a crowd, I will not. Because of my unique position as a pastor, I must get up and get out of my comfort zone and talk.

Character flaws are common to us all and no one should feel bad about having them.

There is a story in the Bible of a man who had a character flaw and was trying to tell God why he was not the right one for a specific assignment.

Exodus 4:10-12 NIV reads, "And Moses said unto the Lord, O my Lord, I am not eloquent, neither heretofore, nor since thou hast spoken unto thy servant: but I am slow of speech, and a slow tongue. And the Lord said unto him, Who hath made man's mouth? Or who maketh the dumb, or deaf, or the seeing, or the blind? Have not I the Lord? Now therefore go, and I will be with thy mouth, and teach thee what thou shalt say."

Moses was dealing with an impediment of speech and he felt like he was not qualified to talk to a pharaoh who was multilingual.

This story shows us that you can have a flaw and God will still use you when you do not rely on your strength, but His.

As you move forward in your leadership journey,

you will learn that your calling will soon overshadow your flaw, and this is what leadership is all about. Just go do it.

Character flaws are common to us all
and no one should feel bad about
having them.

Dr. Deshawn Rouse

One of the ways to bounce back from making a bad decision is to first admit that you made a bad decision. Many leaders sometimes make themselves seem superhuman and whenever they make a mistake, their pride stops them from admitting that they fell short. This kind of behavior sends a message to their people that falling is not acceptable.

If we want our people, to be honest, people need to hear us say, "I have made a bad decision, I have learned something, and I am going to do better". This shows them that failure is okay because it provides a lesson needed for success in their future.

I would describe myself as a servant leader and I have been that my entire life, ever since I could remember. One time while in middle school, I was called Reverend Rouse because I used to preach on the playground to many students as they gathered around before we went back in from recess. I did not know what I was doing at the time, but it came naturally.

On another occasion in my childhood, I was in my neighborhood and I gathered kids around my parents' home in the back yard and gave them snacks while I talked to them about things in life. It was just always in me to be a servant leader.

Many leaders sometimes make themselves seem superhuman and whenever they fall, their pride stops them from admitting that they fell.

Dr. Deshawn Rouse

There is a verse in the Bible that speaks of this. St. Matthew 23:11-12 states "But he that is greatest among you shall be your servant. And whosoever shall exalt himself shall be abased, and he that shall humble himself shall be exalted." Jesus was letting them know that if you are going to be great, you must be a servant. Even Jesus Christ, the Almighty, himself washed people's feet. I believe that when you keep a servant leader's mindset, it keeps you humble as you lead.

We should put people's needs and interests over self. This requires us to demonstrate structure and order. If we are going to go to the next level, order and benchmarks are needed. I have developed this leadership style, through setting benchmarks and goals because I do not think you can be an effective leader without having a clear understanding of where you are going.

CHAPTER 5

BRACE FOR THE IMPACT OF LEADERSHIP

Leadership nuggets covered in this chapter:

❖ The importance of bracing for the impact of leadership.

❖ The journey of leadership and when does it stop.

❖ How leadership style is developed.

Kelvin A. Waites, Sr.

In a previous chapter, I mentioned that for the first ten years of my life I grew up in Harlem, New York, and lived on the 14th floor in the projects with my older brother and my parents. If you were from Harlem or New York, in general, you were expected to be tough. Most days I ran the streets of Harlem with my older brother, Bryan, and my cousin, Steven. Unfortunately, as the youngest and the smallest of the bunch, I would always get the short end of the stick whenever we were involved in something.

We would play games just like regular little boys did. One game that we played consisted of us punching each other in the stomach and whoever flinched or curled up lost. I mean, that was the bottom line. If you flinched or you curled up, you lost. Sounds like fun, right? Even though you had time to brace for the impact of the blow, I can assure you that it still hurt. It just did not hurt as bad because you had time to tense up your muscles and brace yourself for what was about to happen. Leadership, to a certain degree, is the same way.

Bracing ourselves for the impact of leadership is important because we are going to get hit. We get hit with loneliness because the road of leadership is very narrow. As a result, our circles are always small. We can get hit with the fact that people are not going to always agree and support every decision that we make. We will get hit with the fact that we may have to discipline and terminate employees, sometimes people that we have personal relationships with.

As you lead, you will get hit with things that are going on in your personal lives. Just remember that leadership is about carrying your load as well as having to sometimes carry the load of the people that you are charged with leading. You must brace and prepare yourself for the impact because it is not a matter of *if* you will get hit, but a matter of *when* you will get hit.

Even though you had time to brace for
the impact of the blow, I can assure you
that it still hurt.

Kelvin A. Waites, Sr.

Leadership is a journey and should be treated as such. It is a journey because as leaders, we should strive to become the absolute best leaders that we can be. That does not happen overnight. We should continue to improve our skills and our craft by exposing ourselves to new training. Both practical as well as life experiences. No leader should want to be the same leader that they were three years ago or even one year ago.

I know that I handle situations differently today than I did ten years ago. In the past, I made many mistakes and have not always been the best leader that I could have possibly been. However, I can honestly say that I have learned from my mistakes and, in the process, accumulated many tools to put in my toolbox.

As a leader, we should always strive to get better and be better because the people that we are called to lead are always watching. You must be the example that they need for them to see what leadership, professionalism, and fortitude look like. A leader's ability to survive will depend on their ability to stretch, grow, and learn new skills. Leadership is not a sprint, but a marathon that will never end.

Leaders must have vision because having vision gives purpose to the work that we, along with our people do every day. Without that purpose, the people that we lead will not give their best effort because they will have no idea of what their "why" is. In some cases, they will only do the bare minimum or just enough to get by if they do not know the vision. Proverbs 29:18 says that "where there is no vision the people perish." I say that "where there is no vision, your teams, organizations, and your leadership model will perish."

As leaders, it does not do any good to have an airtight plan, mission, or vision if the people you lead are not up to speed on what is going on. Leaders must understand that vision is what connects your people from the present to the future. Not having a vision is just like wandering in the woods at night, in the dark, without even having the moonlight to guide you.

It is not enough just to have a vision, but leaders

Leadership is not a sprint, but a
marathon that will never end.

Kelvin A. Waites, Sr.

must make sure that everyone on their team knows the vision and it is plain. The vision must be made clear and must be specific. We cannot assume and take for granted the fact that everyone has a clear understanding of what the vision is. It is also important for us as leaders, to have vision because vision gives your people hope and something to work towards in the future. If the vision is not relayed to the people, it will be reflected in their work product.

Nasim Al-Hakim, CMB

We all understand the importance of planning and preparation as it relates to disasters, such as a hurricane or tornadoes. But few recognize that leadership roles bring with them disasters that one must prepare for as well. These disasters come with the territory but with preparation, you can survive the impact and successfully overcome it. There are ways that leaders can plan and when disasters arise, they will not catch us by surprise.

> At the highest levels, vision is the most important element in leadership.
>
> *Nasim Al-Hakim, CMB*

Preparation includes knowing your environment, being ahead of what is happening, staying current, and understanding the external and internal elements that could play a part in having an impact of any sort in your leadership journey. Once again, it is important to have a plan and create a "safe" haven for those who you are leading. This is also important because they are looking to you for the answers. They will feel safe knowing that you will lead them through adversity and collectively, you will come out better as a team.

In its simplest form, leadership is a journey that never stops. If you are alive, you can learn, influence, inspire and motivate. With constant life changes, you will also be challenged and tested which will assist you with the experience needed to carry on more responsibilities.

Sight is what we see, vision is what we create, the unseen.

Nasim Al-Hakim, CMB

At the highest levels, vision is the most important element in leadership. It sets the course and tone for others, including yourself to follow. There is a big difference between sight and vision. Sight is what we see, vision is what we create, the unseen. Tangible versus intangible. I think your more effective leaders are more insightful and they are forward-thinking. Also, they know how to create a shared vision, which ultimately increases the cohesiveness of the team. This allows for a more inclusive environment and supports the idea that all opinions matter.

Dr. Deshawn Rouse

The impact of leadership is real, and it can affect those you lead positively or negatively. It will make an impact whether it is in a company, business, marriage, church, city, or region. There is a lot of pressure that comes with an impactful leader.

Sometimes, you are celebrated or criticized, and both can be dangerous if you are not stable mentally. Many people are called to have impactful leadership but are not prepared for what is next.

> The impact of leadership is real, and it can affect those you lead in a positive or negative way.
>
> *Dr. Deshawn Rouse*

When I began pastoring, all my mind was on was seeing lives change. But I soon found out that even though many people were being changed, many people were being upset. I took on a lot of criticism from people saying that I was not real, to say I was leading people astray. That shook me. I could not believe that the people I was trying to help would see me doing so much wrong. But that is what comes when your ministry is being impactful. Sometimes the attacks will come.

If you are deciding to do anything great, you must brace yourself or ask yourself, if you can take the popularity or criticism because it will come. If you are going to be a quintessential leader, then you must prepare for ups and downs. The best thing to do is to not let either go to your head. Stay focused.

Great leaders never stop learning and evolving because they realize leadership is a journey that never stops. The effects of their leadership will not end in retirement or death, but it will continue in the lives of those that they lead. Many people take what they have learned from their leader and leverage that knowledge to carve out their leadership path. As a result, the continuation of that leader's journey is formed.

Now that you are on this journey, you must decide if you want to be an effective leader or just someone in a leadership position. Will leadership be your lifestyle or just your title?

Dr. Deshawn Rouse

Now that you are on this journey, you must decide if you want to be an effective leader or just someone in a leadership position. Is leadership your lifestyle or just your title? If you commit yourself to growth, your leadership will soon become so intertwined with your being that no one will be able to tell the difference between you, the individual, and you, the leader.

In the Bible, there is a verse in Proverbs 29:18 NIV that states: "Where there is no vision, the people perish: but he that keepeth the law, happy is he." This verse clearly states that where there is no vision, the people will perish because there are no parameters for them to keep. Sight is important, but it can limit you and discourage you. Your vision helps you to see beyond limitations by reaching deep down inside and bringing forth that thing that God has placed in you. It also helps you set boundaries, which are important to accomplishing any task.

CHAPTER 6

YOU WERE BUILT FOR THIS

Leadership nuggets covered in this chapter:

❖ The effect of the impostor syndrome on leaders.

❖ Strategies for dealing with the impostor syndrome.

❖ Measuring the effectiveness of leadership.

Kelvin A. Waites, Sr.

As leaders, I believe that we all struggle with the imposter syndrome at one point or another during our leadership journeys. The imposter syndrome is simply when someone doubts their accomplishments and believes that eventually, people will see them as a fake and a fraud. The imposter syndrome causes a leader to believe that they do not belong where they currently are and do not deserve the opportunity that they have.

It is human nature for leaders to go through this and to wonder to themselves if they are capable, ready, and equipped to lead and be successful. I, myself have struggled with the imposter syndrome at every level of my law enforcement career. I struggled with this when I was promoted to Sergeant, Lieutenant, Captain, Deputy Chief of Police, and Chief of Police. I questioned if I belonged and if I was ready for the opportunity that was in front of me.

I suffered from the imposter syndrome, again, when I started my coaching practice, Waites Lifted Life & Leadership Coaching LLC. I wondered if I had what it took to help others achieve their goals and get to the next level. Even though I struggled with imposter syndrome, I was selected to attend the FBI National Academy in Quantico, Virginia in 2012. The significance of my selection was that only about 25% of law enforcement executives from around the world get an opportunity to attend the FBI National Academy.

I questioned why and how I was selected. But, at the end of the day, I believe we give people too much credit. Promotion does not come from people; it comes from God and we are all destined to be where we are at an allotted time while on our leadership journeys. We get the training that we need as well as the experience and continue to put the work in. We are exactly where we should be because we are destined to be here.

The next time you question whether you belong where you are, think about your education and your experience. Realize that, in the natural order of things, God put you where you are for this season because you checked all the boxes and did your part.

You can overcome the imposter syndrome slowly by building up your confidence. Remind yourself that you put in the work. You have the education and you belong exactly where you are. You cannot let that feeling of doubt cripple you as a leader because it will if you let it. Instead, use that fear of failure and doubt to push yourself to the next level.

When I started being more vocal in the community, while representing my police department, I had a phobia regarding talking to crowds of people. It was not the fact that I was afraid to talk in front of people, but I wondered whether they wanted to hear what I had to say. To combat that feeling, I used to go over my resume mentally, just to remind myself that I was qualified to be there. That whatever audience I had sitting in front of me wanted to hear what I had to say.

In addition to that, I believe that on every level that

Promotion does not come from people,
it comes from God and we are all
destined to be where we are at an
allotted time, while on our own
leadership journeys.

Kelvin A. Waites, Sr.

I have personally struggled, was due to the impostor syndrome and the learning curve that I had in front of me. Another thing that I would do to make myself comfortable was to embrace and dig into the policies and procedures of the new organization.

When taking on a new leadership role, I have always sat down and talked to every staff member one-on-one. I have never thought it was a good idea to have big group meetings initially. I recognized that whenever everyone was in one room with me doing the talking and everyone else doing the listening, the dialogue would not travel back and forth as it should. It was one-sided and I missed out on an opportunity to learn about the culture of the organization. Sitting down with each staff member for maybe 15 to 30 minutes, just to see where they are and get a feel for the culture, helped me get a feeling of belonging and assisted me in building rapport.

Ultimately, you conquer the imposter syndrome by training and learning from the gift of experience. Never let anyone outwork you and recognize, at the same time, that you have checked all the boxes. You are where you are because you belong there.

I measure the effectiveness of my leadership by gauging the performance of my people. I look at how well they work together and how well they can accomplish the mission. I do this based on my influence, without me having to tell them, verbatim what to do. Like I said, leadership is about influencing and knowing when you are in tune with the people that you lead.

I also measure the effectiveness of my leadership based on whether my people see and understand the vision. When you are leading at a high level, all you need to do is allude to something that needs to be done without even telling someone exactly what they need to do. You realize that you are onto something when your people know exactly what you are going to say before you even say it. They know what you want before you ask for it and it all just kind of works and it flows in the same direction.

Ultimately, you conquer the imposter
syndrome by training and learning
from the gift of experience.

Kelvin A. Waites, Sr.

At the end of the day, a leader measures the effectiveness of their leadership based on how their people perform when they are not around. Do they carry out the mission like they know the vision or are they crippled with fear when you are not around? Do they freeze up on the battlefield because they are so dependent on you managing them instead of leading them? Being an effective leader takes time, determination, and patience because you do not become effective overnight. It takes a lot of hard work.

Nasim Al-Hakim, CMB

At some point during the journey, all leaders will experience the imposter syndrome. I think that we all will question ourselves to figure out if we are qualified for the role and if others want to hear directly from us. To minimize our effectiveness, we may say to ourselves, "there are others who could do this job" or "their story is just like mine". These statements are not true, because others may have similar skills or stories, but they are not you. Only you can be great at being you.

> When you are a leader you will still have to serve those in your sphere of influence while you battle the imposter syndrome.

Nasim Al-Hakim, CMB

When I experience this, I will go back and look at my body of work and review my resume. Not just my professional resume, but my success resume, as well. I look at what I've overcome, and what I have been able to accomplish despite being raised in a single-parent home in Brooklyn, New York during the crack epidemic in the 1980s.

I grew up where the crime was heavily insulated and many people in my shoes became a statistic. I attended three different high schools and still managed to graduate on time in four years. I moved around a lot and was unable to forge meaningful friendships early on in my life. These are a few of the many challenges that I have experienced during my journey. Nonetheless, I was able to work my way up from an entry-level role to be one of the top real estate finance professionals in the entire country.

Ironically, I still fight with "am I the one?" and you will too. But don't let that stop you from leading. Simply look around at who you have influenced and see how they are doing. If they are successful, it means you are qualified, and you need to be heard because you can impact change in the lives of others. The success of those in your sphere of influence is your proof in combating the impostor syndrome.

When you are a leader, you will still have to serve those in your sphere of influence while you battle the imposter syndrome. These are the times when you reach into your internal toolbox and pull out your courage and tenacity tools. We tend to beat ourselves down because we are creatures of habit and we are never good enough for ourselves. But you must encourage yourself despite those negative voices in your head.

Be quiet and listen for that voice that tells you that

you can do it and put your best foot forward. You need to decide to be confident, courageous, and stand in your authority, no matter what. It will take time and even after years of success you will still have times when you need to rely on those tools and negotiate with yourself to rise to the moment.

Remember, you can lead from the front
and the back.

Nasim Al-Hakim, CMB

When measuring the effectiveness of my leadership, I look at the progression and success of those around me. As the leader, you are at the forefront, focused on building teams and leading those people to new levels. Then you look around and see a person who started in an entry-level position now managing teams. They are mimicking your leadership styles to their people and their people are successful as well. That is when you see the impact of your leadership taking on a life of its own.

You may even find yourself going back to the people that you once led and now you are part of their sphere of influence. You can go to them for questions and they support you on your next level journey. It is not just seeing their successes but also seeing how they can help you grow to be a more effective leader. Remember, you can lead from the front and the back.

Dr. Deshawn Rouse

My struggles with the imposter syndrome arise because of my focus. Whenever I find myself focusing on my character flaws, I begin to question my abilities as a leader. The imposter syndrome is a challenge many leaders will face. I am certain of this because I have had several leaders tell me that they have also questioned why they were chosen. This questioning of oneself happens when leaders are so passionate about the success of those they lead, that they begin to overly critique their abilities to serve them.

Over time, I have found that many leaders in the Bible questioned their roles as leaders. One example of this is found in Jeremiah 1:7 NIV, which reads, "But the Lord said unto me, Say not, I am a child: for thou shalt go to all that I shall send thee, and whatsoever I command thee thou shalt speak."

Before this verse, Jeremiah tries to tell the Lord why he was not qualified to speak on His behalf, but God does not address Jeremiah's abilities in his reply. Instead, God speaks to the authority of leadership that has been given to him. It is like God was saying to Jeremiah, "How dare you question what I have authorized?".

Another leader in the Bible that struggled with the imposter syndrome was Joshua. In Joshua 1:5 NIV, "There shall not any man be able to stand before thee all the days of thy life: as I was with Moses, so I will be with thee: I will not fail thee, nor forsake thee." God reaffirmed to Joshua that the same power that helped Moses lead the people would be the same power to help him lead the people.

> This questioning of oneself happens
> when leaders are so passionate about
> the success of those they lead, that they
> begin to overly critique their abilities
> to serve them.

Dr. Deshawn Rouse

The imposter syndrome will also have you imitating other leaders because you think that if you lead like them, you will get the same results that you see when you look at their leadership. But, if you can just discover yourself, you will see that God has given you a unique way of leading that will bring about greater results.

One of the ways to lead while dealing with the imposter syndrome is to work on your craft, even though you feel heavily influenced by someone else's. Remember the truth of it is you want to develop your gifting. Even though you honor the leaders of the past for what they have shown you, you are living in a different time. Some of the things that worked for them will not work for you.

Many pastors believe in paperback Bibles in hand, but we are living in a more tech society and more modern preachers are walking around with their Apple iPad®. We must understand that we are talking to a more college-based society that are technology savvy. They may feel more modern having their pastor act like their professor. Do not be afraid to be comfortable doing what you need to do to reach this generation.

The effectiveness of one's leadership can be measured by the growth and execution abilities of the people on their team. I believe that these two measurements are also tied to how well you can relate to your people. If your people are failing, it is one thing to blame them, but a great leader will ask "Have I properly and effectively relayed the message?"

Leaders must understand the benefit of having a conversation with their teams to confirm that everyone understands what is being asked of them. If you discover that they are not receiving it the way you said it, then it is your responsibility to find a way to communicate in a way that your people connect with and understand. These are a few powerful questions I use to reinforce communication with my team:

"Can you tell me what you heard?"

"Did you understand what you heard?"

"Will you repeat what you heard me say?"

The effectiveness of one's leadership
can be measured by the growth and
execution abilities of the people on
their team.

Dr. Deshawn Rouse

Every leader should have an effective model of relaying information to those they lead if they want to be successful. The Bible says, "Wisdom is the principal thing; therefore, get wisdom: and with all thy getting get understanding" (Proverbs 4:7 KJV). In schools, students are given aptitude tests to measure their progress and if the child does not comprehend the subject, it can be traced back to how effective the teaching of the subject was.

CHAPTER 7

GET RID OF THE MASK

Leadership nuggets covered in this chapter:

❖ The importance of being an authentic leader.

❖ How vulnerability impacts authentic leadership.

❖ Understanding being a leader, being in a leadership position, and being chosen by people as their leader.

Kelvin Waites

Leaders need to be authentic. If we do not take off our masks, our people will not take theirs off and they will not follow us. They may do just enough to get by based on their professionalism, but if your people sense that you are not being authentic, they will not run through walls for you. You must be authentic so that your people will commit to your leadership. It is impossible to get your team to commit to the mission of the organization if they lack trust in the person leading them. Trust is built when people know who you are.

Many leaders shy away from telling their people the truth. It is important to take the mask off if you want them to follow you. You must be the same person who was invited to the party in the first place. You must be real with yourself in taking your mask off. We must be able to talk to our people and tell them the truth, as it relates to their work performance.

For example, if someone has deficiencies or challenges, instead of ignoring it and blowing it off, pull that person to the side and say, "Hey, I appreciate all of your hard work, but I need you to work on A, B, and C."

Of course, when they are exceptional, it is your job as their leader to be their biggest cheerleader.

I believe that on the journey of leadership every leader, at some point, will have to make themselves vulnerable to their people. I believe that to be an effective leader you must be who you say you are.

For a long time, I was results-driven. I did not care about what was going on in my employees' personal lives. All I cared about was getting the job done. I did not want to hear any drama in the workplace.

You must be authentic so that your
people will commit to your leadership.

Kelvin A. Waites, Sr.

I feared that my employees' personal lives would spill over into the workplace and hurt the work product. I would often say "hey, don't bring any drama up in here." I wanted people to keep all of the extra stuff away from work. I did not want to hear anything from my employees unless it had to do with work and in return, all I received from them was the status quo.

It was not until I learned that I had to take more of an interest in the people that I was responsible to lead that I saw positive results.

I finally figured it out, after attending a leadership conference in Dallas, Texas at Bishop T.D. Jakes' church. At that conference, I learned that if my people knew that I was genuinely concerned and cared about their lives away from work, then they would run through walls for me at work. They finally embraced my leadership when they saw that I had compassion for them, had empathy, and support them.

Once I had supported them in handling those housekeeping issues, my people understood and embraced the philosophy that I could be vulnerable to them. I learned that I could show empathy toward my team while pushing them to their next level of excellence.

All leaders should recognize that meekness is not a weakness. It is a strength.

I believe people choose me as their leader because they know I have a vision. It is a vision that I do not mind sharing and pushing towards. They know that I will push them to reach their full potential as well. People choose me as their leader because they know that I care and I want the best for them, as well as the organization. They also know that I am always going to do the right thing.

When people realize and have confidence in the fact that you are always going to do the right thing, they will follow you. Whether it negatively impacts them or not, they will support your vision. They may not always agree with your decisions, but they will respect them.

Over the years of my professional career, I have had

Doing the right thing all the time is the
key to a leader's success, even when
doing the right thing hurts.

Kelvin A. Waites, Sr.

the opportunity to promote personal friends that I have known for fifteen to twenty years. I knew their families and for some, I was even there when their children were born. These were times when my integrity as a leader would be tested.

Would I promote this person based on our friendship or would I evaluate them in terms of what they bring to the table and what was best for the organization?

No one would have said anything if I had promoted them, but I knew I would have to live with the decision for the rest of my life. In every instance, the right thing to do, no matter how difficult, was to promote the person that I knew was the best fit for the position and organization at the time, regardless of my relationship with them.

There will be times when you will have to make tough decisions, and this is when you must do what is in the best interest of your team and the organization.

Remember, even if your decisions do not have an

individual impact on your people, they are always looking to see if you are making decisions based on what is best for the whole or what is best for you and a few. When they see you are willing to sacrifice yourself for the team, they will believe in you and your vision. Doing the right thing all the time is the key to a leader's success, even when doing the right thing hurts.

Nasim Al-Hakim, CMB

There is a difference between being real and being true. Being real, to a certain point, is subjective. I am real until I am compromised and at that point, "realness" is out the window. Being true is being true to yourself. This transitions into when you allow people to see who you are. It means that you accept the truth about who lies within you.

> When you are vulnerable, you are
> open, and I think that being vulnerable
> makes you human.

Nasim Al-Hakim, CMB

It can be tough to accept the truth about yourself. It does not matter if you failed a lot of times in life or you did not accomplish what you wanted to in some spaces, you must accept who you are. And I think that when people view a leader or anybody who could accept themselves for who they are, it allows them to feel more comfortable expressing their true selves as well.

Vulnerable is not a negative word. When you are vulnerable, you are open, and I think that being vulnerable makes you human. I do not think there is anybody that I know personally who has mastered everything they set out to accomplish. Thus, it is important to champion or master what you can and learn from your previous failures. It is your failures that will ultimately propel you to your successes. I must remind myself that it is not about how many times I failed; it is about how many times I got back up to fight.

If there is not an inspection of what you are expecting, you are probably not going to see the results that you are looking for.

Nasim Al-Hakim, CMB

Being in a leadership role does not mean people will follow you. You must display the type of leadership that people want to follow. I am a leader that focuses on inspiring my team and leading by example. I support and assist in their growth. I help them to create their vision. I even have a shared vision with them as well. More than anything else, I hold them accountable.

The accountability piece is something many leaders lose sight of and think that doing their job as leaders is enough. I think that you must hold others accountable. Being able to not just be there for them, 43but make sure they stay on that path to get to where they need to get to. That is the key to the accountability piece that we tend to leave out. If you are not holding others accountable, you are not preparing them for a life of effective leadership.

In my leadership journey, I have learned that there is something quite simple when it comes to accountability, and that is you must inspect what you expect. If there is not an inspection of what you are expecting, you are probably not going to see the results that you are looking for. And you will not be able to execute your plans or goals.

Dr. Deshawn Rouse

You must be authentic if you are going to be a successful leader. You should be true to yourself. So many people who are leaders and they do it because of the position and their hearts are not in it. They put on a facade in front of the people like they are concerned and passionate, but behind closed doors, they could care less about the people. I think that people can feel that energy, it gives off a vibe that someone is not all in. Leaders like this tend to come off as fake to those that encounter their leadership.

> You should be authentic in your
> leadership as well, because sooner or
> later, people will figure you out.

Dr. Deshawn Rouse

Many politicians come off genuine when they give you the political smile and handshake. One of the things many African-Americans liked about U.S. President, John F. Kennedy when he was running for President back in the '60s, was the feeling of honesty they got from watching him hold their babies. He would take time to connect to what was most important to them. In other words, people felt he was authentic.

You should be authentic in your leadership as well because sooner or later, people will figure you out.

People need to see a side of you that is human, but at the same time, they need to see a leader who is still operating and moving them forward. There is a story in the Bible where Jesus got into a boat and pushed off from the seashore. He spoke to the crowd that was still on the shore from the boat. Jesus was close enough to be heard by them but far enough to not be physically touched by them. (St. Luke 5)

I love this story because it is a great example of how important it is for your people to hear your voice, without the ability to touch you in a way you should not be touched. They should see your vulnerability, but they should not be able to touch your vulnerable places.

Too much access can have dangerous impacts on a leader, such as burnout and being overwhelmed. Every leader should have times when they can just pull away, regroup, and come back with full authority to help the people they are assigned to.

The authority that many leaders have can sometimes cause them to confuse being in charge with being a leader. These are two vastly different things.

For instance, if someone is sitting in the front seat of a car, does it make them the owner of that car?

No, it does not.

Therefore, if your people have placed you in a leadership position, then you must do your best to uphold the trust they have placed in you.

Dr. Deshawn Rouse

People will not choose someone as their leader simply because they are in a leadership role, they choose someone as their leader because they view them as someone they can trust, depend on, and can follow without embarrassment. It is like when people choose a certain restaurant they want to go to, they look at the letter on the door to see if they can be trusted.

I teach the leaders in my church that you do not become someone's leader, but someone must choose you to be their leader and that is an honorable thing. We live in a society, especially the political arena, where people choose their leaders. Therefore, if your people have placed you in a leadership position, then you owe it to them to uphold the trust they have placed in you.

CHAPTER 8

EVERY LEADER HAS A TOOLBOX

Leadership nuggets covered in this chapter:

❖ The tools every leader needs.

❖ How to use your tools to benefit those that you lead.

❖ The impact of culture on your leadership abilities and effectiveness.

Kelvin A. Waites, Sr.

Leadership tools are a must for every leader, and three significant tools that every leader should have in their toolboxes are courage, determination, and sacrifice.

Leaders need courage because, at the end of the day, the buck stops with us. We make decisions that impact the lives of others daily and sometimes it can be a matter of life or death. Many of those decisions will go against the grain and everyone will not be happy about them. Some decisions may be considered outside of the box and people will challenge you by saying, "We have always done things this way." At times like this, courage is that tool that will enable a leader to stand behind those unpopular decisions.

As a leader, you will have to take calculated risks and it takes courage to do that. You will not always be able to predict the outcome of those risks, but with courage, you can hold yourself accountable and move forward. Courage is an asset and it is one of the most valuable tools a leader can have in their toolbox.

Another tool is determination. Leaders should have the fortitude to push towards their vision. I have encountered leaders who use the idea of low morale to justify why their team is not following their agendas and pushing through difficult times. However, the truth is that they lacked the determination to stay focused and committed to the mission amid challenges. A leader should not be intimidated or influenced by false propaganda that is being broadcasted by disgruntled employees or employees who are afraid of change.

While many different things will come into play to try to discourage us, we must keep our eyes on the prize, remain determined, and stay focused on the mission.

The final basic tool a leader needs in their toolbox is

> While many different things will come
> into play to try to discourage us, we
> must keep our eyes on the prize,
> remain determined and stay focused
> on the mission.

Kelvin A. Waites, Sr.

sacrifice. We should acknowledge and act on the fact that it cannot just be about us, but it is about the team. Our job as leaders is to serve and we should be mindful of this in our roles and ensure that the people we lead have everything they need to be successful.

It does not matter if you are starting a brand-new toolbox or if you have an old one. Make sure that you have courage, determination, and sacrifice in it.

Over time, you will accumulate tools by way of good, bad, and ugly experiences that you have in life. Those tools you acquire will become a benefit to others when you know exactly what you have, and you are willing to let someone else use or borrow those tools.

Just like a helpful handyman will reach into their toolbox to give a hammer to someone who needs to nail something down, a leader must be willing to reach in their toolbox and willfully provide their employees with what they need to nail down their tasks as well.

Our toolboxes are full of various experiences that can be referenced to help the people that we lead along the way. Good leaders share what they have in their toolboxes to help and assist everyone around them. If we are not using our tools and experiences to lift others, then we are not demonstrating good leadership.

Maybe you have experienced not getting the promotion that you wanted. You could share with others how you were able to overcome that and get better promotion. Or you could have experienced being terminated and you can witness to others the steps you took to move forward. Whatever experiences you may have endured throughout your life, personally or professionally, they have a place in your toolbox.

We should freely use our tools to mentor other people when they come to us saying, "I'm working on my career development and was wondering what you thought about this or that." If you are leading at a high level, you are using and sharing the tools in your toolboxes to help others and to serve as a reference for yourself, as well.

Culture also plays a major role as it relates to your leadership. The culture that you create, entertain, and allow within your organization reflects on your leadership. If you foster a culture of the "good ole boy system" that doesn't promote hiring, promoting, and disciplining based on merit, the morale of your team or organization will be low and harm your leadership.

Here is an example of the "good ole boy system". "Hey, let's just hire Bobby because that's Sarah's son and he is a good ole boy."

Bobby may not have the minimum education or the experience required for the job but, because his family is plugged in, he has an unfair advantage. Allowing or facilitating this type of culture will have a devastating impact on your organization over time.

The culture of your organization is important and as the leader, you will set the tone for everyone else. Because you set the tone, it is extremely important that everyone, from top to bottom, within your organization, buys into that culture. There are, however, several factors that can make this a very tough thing to accomplish at times.

One of the greatest threats to a healthy culture is CHANGE! If we are transparent and honest with ourselves, we will all admit that nobody likes change, even if it makes sense and is good for us. It is a leader's job to be the change agent within their organization. Not by driving the change down your

---

The culture of your organization must
be one that allows every employee to
be creative, as well as entertain an
environment that allows for diversity.

Kelvin A. Waites, Sr.

people's throats, but by helping them to understand how the change will benefit them individually as well as professionally while increasing the overall effectiveness of the organization.

Generational gaps also play a major role in an organization's culture. Sometimes, what I call the "old salty dogs" of an organization, refuse to come to terms with the fact that the millennials play a vital role in the workforce. They are here to stay!

On the flip side, some millennials refuse to acknowledge that some of those same "old salty dogs" within the organization can teach them a thing or two about loyalty and integrity, as well as share with them their encyclopedias of institutional knowledge that is beneficial to all.

These two groups play a major role within the culture of many organizations. If the two groups can find a way to meet in the middle, their organization would flourish and run like a well-oiled machine. It is up to the leader to assist both groups in finding that common ground that values everyone's strengths and works to complement and compensate for each other's weaknesses. In other words, "where you are weak, I am strong!"

It is 2020 and we must get away from facilitating and entertaining toxic cultures within our families, workspaces, and organizations if we are going to move forward. If not, the morale of our families, companies, and organizations will be low and we will hurt our overall effectiveness and productivity.

The culture of your organization must allow every employee to be creative and entertains an environment that fosters diversity and inclusion. As the leaders of our organizations, we should be certain that our organizations are hiring and promoting based on merit. It is not enough to just have the right culture in place, we must also take the appropriate measures to protect that culture.

We can protect our culture by putting in place policies and procedures that reinforce the best practices within our industries or professions and the culture of our organizations. The culture within an organization will always reflect its leadership.

When it is all said and done, the leadership must take on the responsibility of defining their brand. If you do not define your brand, your customers, clients, citizens, etc. will define it for you, and if that happens, it may not represent the brand the way you want it to. Always ask yourself, "What are people saying about the brand of my company or organization when I'm not in the room?".

Nasim Al-Hakim, CMB

Some of the key tools of leadership are energy, enthusiasm, confidence, resilience, empathy, self-assurance, humility, servitude, courage, support, and ownership. No one tool is better than the other. However, energy is particularly important.

Energy comes from your physical, spiritual, and mental wellness and it is a tool to help you execute efficiently with the other tools.

Having tools in your toolbox is not enough. You must use those tools. It does no good if you have the tools and do not leverage them. You leverage them by living in your purpose.

> Having tools in your toolbox is not enough. You must use those tools… You leverage them by living in your purpose.
>
> *Nasim Al-Hakim, CMB*

If you say you are a carpenter and you fix houses, then use your hammer, jackhammer, and your wrench. When you get out there, people expect to see the carpentry tools they do not expect to see a toothbrush.

All in all, you must use your tools so others can see how it is done. Setting the example is important.

Culture is important because it is the breeding ground for growth and leadership.

There is a difference between diversity and inclusion. This has been a big topic in recent years.

What does it look like in your eyes?

In some respect, we've grown a lot since the 60's as it pertains to diversity. Although it is not at the point many of us want to see it, it has grown some with plenty of runway for improvement. However, we have a long road to inclusion. Just because you see a diverse culture, does not mean that it is an inclusive culture.

A shared culture creates synergy and
formulates a unified foundation.

Nasim Al-Hakim, CMB

When you have a shared culture, you live and breathe that culture. It is important to include it in your leadership vision as well. Thus, solidarity will exist.

The culture does not belong to the leader, it is shared by the entire team, and it fits into the overall vision of the organization. This makes it easier for everyone to believe in the culture and the mission.

A shared culture creates synergy and formulates a unified foundation. Hence, everyone knows what to expect because they know the culture. They understand their roles and how that role fits into the overall mission.

Dr. Deshawn Rouse

The very first tool you should have in your toolbox is love. Love was the overall message that Christ demonstrated throughout His mission on earth.

Being a pastor, I must demonstrate this wholeheartedly with everyone I encounter, especially my congregants. I am the Christlike example that they need to follow in using the tool of love.

Sometimes this tool can be challenging due to the ups and downs of life that people go through, but rest assured, love never fails. If love is not in your toolbox, make sure you add it.

Tenacity is also a tool every leader needs. You must keep going even when you come home and feel like things did not go right at the office.

Dr. Deshawn Rouse

Another tool is one that I mentioned in a previous chapter and that is character. The character tool is remaining consistent even though everyone else is doing something to the contrary. You know your moral compass and what you have been called to do.

Tenacity is also a tool that every leader needs. You

must keep going even when you come home and feel like things did not go right at the office. You must shake it off and go back at it again tomorrow and get the desired results.

Love, character, and tenacity are three tools you need in your toolbox to lead people effectively. When they see you operating in love for other people, displaying good character in tough times, and taking tenacious actions, then they will likely model that same behavior when they face challenges in their future. Remember, if God has placed people under you, then He wants them to learn something from you for a future event in their own life.

One such example that I had was my pastor who suffered a massive heart attack and became an amputee in both legs. Despite all the odds being against him, he continued coming to church to preach and teach his congregation. Seeing this behavior from him led me to believe that no matter what comes up in my life, I should continue pressing forward. This experience has stayed with me throughout my 21 years of pastoring my church.

Culture plays a big role in leadership and I am going to come from the mindset of the millennials, seeing things differently from the previous generations. A lot of leaders have a hard time relating to the millennial generation. I believe you must be able to adapt to their verbiage, their ways, their mannerisms, and their work ethic if you are going to begin relating to this generation.

Decades ago, employers wanted their employees to work an eight, ten, or twelve-hour shift with very few breaks. But today, many of our large companies, such as Amazon and Google have realized that you must become innovative and provide accommodations to support your employee's needs and productivity.

If you want to see effectiveness and
productivity in the culture that we live
in today, then we must learn to employ
new mindsets.

Dr. Deshawn Rouse

Examples of this progressive approach include allowing employees to take sleep breaks at work, providing fitness equipment at workstations, and setting up onsite daycare services for the children of their employees.

If you want to see effectiveness and productivity in the culture that we live in today, then we must learn to employ new mindsets.

CHAPTER 9

ASSEMBLE A TRIBE

Leadership nuggets covered in this chapter:

❖ The importance of having a team you can trust.

❖ The dangers of having a team that thinks the same.

❖ Celebrating the wins of those you lead.

Kelvin A. Waites, Sr.

No leader has all the answers. Therefore, it is necessary to have a team around you that you can trust to share their perspective with you. Your team should not consist only of people that agree with you all the time though. The people on your team should be able to tell you the truth, even when they think that it is going to be contrary to your thought process.

It is equally important to have people around you and in your camp that you can trust to not give out critical information at inappropriate times. You need the type of people around you that would never undermine the mission and vision that you have for your organization.

Now, this circle of trust will not create itself and it will not happen overnight. Leaders must be mentors and create an environment for people to feel comfortable in sharing their true feelings, insight, and perspectives. You will create this type of atmosphere when you ask for and welcome feedback, whether it is positive or negative. Additionally, your ability to handle constructive criticism, professionally and maturely also contributes to creating a safe environment for your team.

This group of trusted individuals must know, accept, and believe in the mission of your organization. You need to be able to trust and believe in them to be the Drum Majors of your organizations. They will keep everyone else in step and aligned with the goals and objectives outlined by your leadership for your organization. Trust and believe that if the Drum Majors have not bought into what the program calls for and they are marching offbeat, everyone else will be offbeat as well.

> Leaders must be mentors and create the environment for people to feel comfortable in sharing their true feelings, insight, and perspectives.

> *Kelvin A. Waites, Sr.*

The last thing that any leader should want to be is like the Emperor in the short tale written by Hans Christian Anderson, titled "The Emperor's New Clothes." The moral of the story was that pride and the fear of telling the Emperor the truth caused the Emperor to be embarrassed because he walked around his kingdom naked. All the trusted people around him knew he was naked, but nobody had enough integrity or courage to tell him.

This is not the kind of people that leaders need around them. You need to build a team around you that will tell you the truth no matter what the consequences are.

I want a group of leaders and decision-makers sitting at the table with me that think differently than I do because there is power in diversity. I believe in the saying that "just because you're right doesn't mean I'm wrong". There are many ways to do things. As leaders, we cannot be overly sensitive when people disagree with us and have a different perspective.

I find beauty and an advantage in having a diverse group of people to give me their honest feedback and counsel daily. As a result, I and my organization are better, stronger, and more efficient. Of course, everyone involved knows that I will make the final decision at the end of the day, but their feedback, perspective, and their wisdom certainly assist me in making the most educated and informed decision that I can.

Throughout my career, I have had the opportunity to work for a Sheriff, two Chiefs of Police, and a District Attorney. I have been blessed during my career to have always been able to voice my opinion and perspective respectfully and tactfully. I was able to do this without having to worry about consequences or retaliation because I had a different perspective or opinion on something. I did this knowing that a final decision would be made, possibly opposite of my position, but I was still able to communicate how I felt.

Once the decision was made, whatever it was, I took my marching orders out to the people that I was charged with leading and said, "This is what we have to do." I was able to take ownership of the decision because I knew my voice was heard and my team did not need to hear me say anything contrary to the decision set forth. Saying things like "well this is what our fearless leader wants us to do, or this is what they want us to do", is the type of behavior that creates dissension among the ranks.

Once I was elevated to a higher position of leadership, I wanted to duplicate that kind of atmosphere because I knew that it made an organization better in two different ways.

Number one, diversity in every form is a strength. Number two, creating that kind of atmosphere empowers employees to think outside of the box and bring their creative ideas to the forefront, instead of sitting on them.

If the people sitting at the table with you cannot tell the truth about what they are feeling based on their perspective, they should not be sitting at the table with you.

I have never been afraid or intimidated to see any of the people that I lead, win. I have always believed that when my employees excel and do great things, it is a credit to our team, our organization, our culture, our brand, and my effectiveness as a leader. When they win, I have done my job and we all win. My job is to mentor them and provide the necessary training they need to continue winning.

Before I was even thinking about becoming a Police Chief, I worked for the District Attorney's Office as an investigator. My former District Attorney was a gentleman named Greg Hembre. Mr. Hembre is now a Senator for the State of South Carolina and he believed that I would be a Chief of Police one day, even before I did. He planted a seed in me that helped me grow to where I am today.

I never considered being a Chief of Police until he and I were eating lunch one day and he said "Kelvin, I

As leaders, we cannot be overly
sensitive when people disagree with us
and have a totally different perspective.

Kelvin A. Waites, Sr.

know that you're not going to be here very long because you are going to be a Chief of Police one day." He went on to tell me that if there was anything that he could do to help me along the way to let him know. Whether it was training or advice, he was always there for me.

As leaders, we all need to be that type of person for our people. We need to be able to put them in a position or mindset to win and see the greatness in them, even before they see it. Just like we raise our children to go out into the world and be great while making sure that they have everything that they need to succeed, we should do the same for the people that we lead.

Nasim Al-Hakim, CMB

When I think of a leader and the team around him, I think of the saying, "iron sharpens iron". You cannot sharpen a knife with wood, or with cotton, or with paper, right? A leader's tribe is important because of the trust you have in them to know that you are equally bringing your best to the table. That trust allows you to be honest and transparent.

Often leaders will surround themselves with people who are not honest with them. To spare the feelings of the leader, the people around them will only say things that align with the leader's perspective, even if they have a different view. This type of behavior prevents growth for the team and the leader.

> When you have people around you that
> you trust, they are those who will
> support you for who you are.

Nasim Al-Hakim, CMB

When you have people around you that you trust, they are those who will support you for who you are. They will also support who you want and who you need to be. This is important.

The demise of a leader will occur if everyone at that

table thinks exactly like them. Many bring in a lot of like-minded people because it feels good. It supports how they feel, and the leader thinks it makes their transition smoother. This creates a comfort zone for the leader which ultimately breeds limitations.

However, change and growth will not come from being comfortable. Growth only comes from exposure to different perspectives, viewpoints, and a diversity of ideas. Because of this, I do not believe in having everyone at the table that is like-minded.

Growth only comes from exposure to different perspectives, viewpoints, and a diversity of ideas.

Nasim Al-Hakim, CMB

We all bring something special, different gifts, and we have different toolboxes. And if you are building a house, and you only bring five plumbers to the table, that house will not get built. If you only bring five roofers to the table, the house will not get built. If you only bring five HVAC contractors to the table, the house is not going to get built either.

But, if you bring a plumber, HVAC person, a roofer, a contractor, and a cement person, your chances of getting the house built would increase. The same is true in leadership, the more diverse thinking you have on your team, the more it will increase your chances of accomplishing your goals.

The whole goal of leadership is to see the people around you win. I always want to see my team win because when one of us wins; we all win collectively. No matter the outcome, we have each other and the opportunity to win or fail forward.

Dr. Deshawn Rouse

It is especially important to have a team that you can trust when you are a visionary. As a leader, sharing pertinent information and seeing that the information is executed well is a win for the team. A leader does not want to see it fail or become manipulative with what you have told them. You do not need people on your team that would try to hurt you, but you want people who will take what you said and run with it. In Habakkuk 2:2 KJV states: "And the Lord answered me, and said, Write the vision, and make it plain upon tables, that he may run that readeth it."

> It is important to have different perspectives and even though you are the leader, you can listen to everything and choose the best one.
>
> *Dr. Deshawn Rouse*

And so, the desire is when you have a vision, you have people who hear it and see it and run with it. You want them to accomplish it instead of trying to sabotage it. Having people that believe in your vision is a key factor too. These are the people who when they see you getting tired, will keep your hands lifted through encouragement. You must assemble a tribe that has your back.

I do not want everyone at the table to be just like me. You must have people at the table that, while they believe in your vision, will still be able to express themselves.

There are some ideas that I think I had, for example, writing a book. There are many ideas that you can have that seem correct to you, but when you get a publisher, they show you a better way. Even though you came up with the main idea, some people can assist you and make your vision more effective. Just because you have the book in your head does not mean you know how to effectively put it down on paper, such as spelling and correct grammar and such.

So, if everyone at the table thinks like you, you are only going to produce the things that your limited thinking will bring to pass. It is important to have different perspectives and even though you are the leader, you can listen to everything and choose the best one. You need people who can express themselves and make you go back and reshape ideas and do something different to be more effective.

Every leader should want their people to win. I believe it makes a leader look good when the people on his team are winning. A mature leader understands he or she does not always have to win. You do not have to be recognized for everything. The very fact that the team is winning means you are winning. I believe you should advocate for people to win and never be intimidated by them.

Whenever a leader gets intimidated by his or her team winning, he begins to smother their gifts. You begin to fan out their flames. The thing they could do to bring attention to you, your company, your church, etc. will never happen.

Every leader should want their people
to win.

Dr. Deshawn Rouse

I have a pastor in my church, Jeron Langley, who is an African American male and fluent in speaking Spanish. He can talk to the Spanish community for our church. I cannot speak Spanish, but I applaud him because he knows how to. It is a plus for both of us. I encourage him to maximize that gift because it makes all of us look good.

In other words, the entire team is winning. I believe when we have everyone at the table doing their own thing and they are winning; it is a plus. Many people are afraid to applaud their people under them. They are afraid the people will get up and leave. If you treat people right, they will never leave you, no matter where they are. They will thank you for your mentorship.

CHAPTER 10

THEY LONG FOR YOUR LEADERSHIP

Leadership nuggets covered in this chapter:

❖ Understanding what is needed from you as a leader.

❖ Avoiding the pitfalls of leading from your comfort zone.

❖ How to pull the best out of those that you lead.

Kelvin A. Waites, Sr.

If the people that we lead are going to be successful, they are going to need a few things from us. First and foremost, the people that we lead need us to show up. Our presence means everything to our people. We must be visible leaders and not be what I call "M.I.L.", which stands for Missing in Leadership.

The people that we are called to lead deserve a leader that they can feel, smell, and touch. One who is accessible to them when they need them the most. If you are going to be a successful leader within your organization, no matter what it is, you must be someone whom your people believe in and someone who they can trust. For them to feel this way about you, not only should they see you, but they should feel you and your presence. Leadership is not something that you can put on autopilot.

The second thing they need from us, for them to be successful, is for us to encourage them. As leaders, it is easy for us to bark out orders all day. We should not only talk about our vision and how we want to see things done, but more importantly, we should encourage the people that we were called to lead. We must push them in the right direction and tell them they can do it. It is our job, as leaders, to make sure that they have all the tools that they need and the support from us that will allow them to go out and be great.

The third thing that our people need from us, whether they know it or not, is that they need us to show them instead of just telling them. We cannot just tell them how to work hard. We must show them. We cannot tell them that we want them to treat our customers, clients, and citizens with the highest level of dignity and respect if we are not treating them the same way. It is our responsibility to be an example and model for them.

Finally, we cannot tell the people that we are

Leadership is not something that you
can put on autopilot.

Kelvin A. Waites, Sr.

charged with leading that we want them to be team players if we are not playing by the same set of rules. Yes, we depend on our people and we need and expect a lot from them, but we must hold up our end of the bargain. Showing up for your people, encouraging them, and not just telling them but showing them, can make all the difference in the world for your people and your organization. Your effectiveness as a leader as well as your organization depends on it.

It is important for leaders not to let themselves fall

into the trap of being content or being stuck in a comfort zone. We must continuously be in a posture that allows us to stretch and grow as leaders. When I use the term stretch and grow, I am talking about an individual challenging themselves every day to become better people individually, as well as becoming more efficient in their craft. If you are not stretching and growing, your leadership will get stale.

Your people will question your leadership. You must step up your game because, ultimately, it is your job as a leader to make sure, at the end of the day, that you are inspiring and motivating your people. You cannot start thinking that you have it all figured out because when you do you are surely setting yourself up for failure.

Someone once said that "If you are standing still then you are falling behind." When it is all said and done, it is not good for leaders to be overly comfortable and just occupy their comfort zones. We need to "get comfortable being uncomfortable." Laws, best practices, the workforce, company policies, and procedures are constantly changing, and all leaders should always have their heads on a swivel and an ability to be flexible.

I have learned through my own experience that leadership calls for us to challenge the norms and push the envelope daily. We must ensure that we do not get trapped in our comfort zones because, if we are not stretching our limits then we are not growing.

As leaders, pulling the absolute best out of your people is somewhat of an art. The challenge is being subtle and discrete about it to the point that they do not even know that you are pushing their buttons. To accomplish this, leaders must bring that fire and enthusiasm to the workplace with them every single day. Not just Monday, Wednesday, or Friday, but every day you have an opportunity to walk in the door with an energy that is contagious to everyone around you.

Leaders must show up ready to rock and roll,

Having positive energy will cause your people to want to follow you because it is contagious.

Kelvin A. Waites, Sr.

realizing that your "attitude has everything to do with your attitude" and that you set the tone. Another way to get the best out of your people without them knowing is to require and expect excellence from them until it is the norm. Be their biggest cheerleader when they do well and address issues and challenges as they come up.

Do not blow off opportunities to get better,

assuming or anticipating that real issues will fix themselves. When we ignore issues and concerns, acting like it is all good, we are not doing anyone any favors. Being silent about problems because you do not want to rock the boat or hurt anybody's feelings is not healthy for you, your company, or your organization.

To get the best out of your people, you must be honest about where they are as it relates to the expectations of your common goal or mission for your organization. We owe it to our people, to be honest. Just remember that if you bring that spark, that fire, and enthusiasm to work every day, that is half of the battle. Having positive energy will cause your people to want to follow you because it is contagious.

Nasim Al-Hakim, CMB

For my people to be successful they need for me to continue the path of personal development. Once again, I think if you are in a comfort zone, you are stagnant and you are not personally growing, then you cannot lead them to their destinations.

Personal development comes to mind and supports in the way of holding them accountable. They need me to help them to see their/our vision and execute on it. They need me to push them harder than anyone else can. They also need to see me walking the walk. This shows them how it is done and lays a foundation of consistency in their routine.

> Reach for higher goals to avoid being in
> the pitfall of being in a comfort zone.
>
> *Nasim Al-Hakim, CMB*

Finally, they need me to set high expectations for them to reach. In doing so, they can elevate above their competitors and be victorious. Remember, there is no growth for a leader who only leads from their comfort zone.

This is especially true in sales when people have good commission months. They tend to slack off because they feel like they had a productive month. As a result, they put themselves in cruise control for the following month. The third month comes, and they are like, "wow, I have to work harder now to get back to the level I was before". But the key is that if they had kept on working, they would not have gotten into their comfort zone in one month.

We must be conscious of not allowing external factors to slow us down because we have achieved our goals and more importantly when we reach a comfort zone. When you reach a goal, it means that you need to exceed your expectations by setting your goals a little bit higher so you could work harder to accomplish them. Reach for higher goals to avoid being in the pitfall of a comfort zone.

You can pull the best out of people by setting expectations for them. Setting goals for the team and them individually push them to drive for the results. Since the leader steers the vision of the entire team, a leader can help to push the team's visions further and show them that they can achieve more. This results in the entire team achieving success collectively and individually.

It is also important to allow them to get to the next step. As a leader, you should be able to delegate. I think leaders struggle with delegation because we tend to want to be hands-on way more than we should. If you trust that you have led them correctly, then you should be able to delegate the task to your team and let them be the champions.

The art of delegation is overlooked and underused by many in leadership.

Nasim Al-Hakim, CMB

When you do this, you are creating more time for other tasks that you have while empowering your team to become leaders as well.

The art of delegation is overlooked and underused by many in leadership. But I have worked to master the art of delegation and I have empowered many to be leaders along my journey.

Dr. Deshawn Rouse

I love the word successful because in that word is another word... success. According to the dictionary, success means the degree or measure of succeeding. You must-have bits and pieces of success following each other.

When I was able to build a new home, I told my wife that I was glad that my kids were able to see it. Not just the finished product, but the entire process. I knew that seeing stages involved in getting to the finished product would give them an appreciation for the hard work that goes into achieving their goals.

I knew that seeing stages involved in getting to the finished product would give them an appreciation for the hard work that goes into achieving their goals.

Dr. Deshawn Rouse

I believe that if a true leader wants his or her people to be successful, then the leader will allow them to look in and see the days they cried and were frustrated. Let them see how they came back swinging again and again. Your people must have a mixture of sunshine and rain.

Leadership is a journey and there are no comfort zones along a journey. Whenever you get into your comfort zone, you are not learning anything else. You have become closed and withdrawn and that will produce stagnation. Coming out of your comfort zone will cause you to rebalance yourself.

Often, people who lose a limb in their body gain strength in the other limb that remains. When you come out of your comfort zone, you lose that comfortability you had, and you must learn to gain strength in other areas.

Leadership is a journey and there are
no comfort zones along a journey.

Dr. Deshawn Rouse

In pastoring, I see many gifts in people. One of the ways I pull it out of them is to assign them to do certain things they are reserved to do. Things such as decorating, doing different assignments out of their comfort zone, and speaking in front of the congregation. Usually, after they do it, they get a good response. They would tell me, "Pastor, I knew I could do it, but I was too scared, and thank you for pushing me." Some people must be pushed to fly.

CHAPTER 11

THE ARENA

Leadership nuggets covered in this chapter:

❖ Handling the stress and pressure associated with leadership.

❖ The meaning and importance of a sphere of influence.

❖ Establishing connections as a new leader.

Kelvin A. Waites, Sr.

Handling the stress and pressure associated with being in the middle of the arena often makes me think about the movie "Gladiator." When Russell Crowe was standing in the middle of the arena some people were cheering for him, others were cheering against him, and some did not care what happened to him either way. Despite that, he stood ready with confidence because he knew he belonged.

Russell Crowe standing in that arena is the equivalent of the attention and spotlight that you are exposed to as a leader every day. Standing in the spotlight of leadership is not easy and can sometimes feel like a curse instead of a blessing. This is true of leaders on every level. At some time or another, we all must give ourselves a gut check to make sure that we are mentally prepared to deal with the stress of the arena.

In a previous chapter, I shared with you tips for dealing with imposter syndrome. One of those tips also applies to the stress and pressure of being in the middle of the arena. You must first acknowledge that you belong there. Recognize that you were called, and you are destined to be exactly where you are at this appointed time.

My dad used to tell me as a child that "we are all

actors in God's production." If that is the case then we must play our roles to the best of our ability, knowing that God would not put more on us than we can bear. Not only did he put you in the arena to lead, but he equipped you with everything that you will need to get the job done.

While handling the stress and pressure of the arena, it is important to not get caught up with listening to the naysayers. Be careful of the noise in the arena because it is only a distraction. As I shared earlier, self-care is especially important to the overall success of leaders and when it comes to dealing with the pressures of standing in the middle of the arena, tuning out the noise is an essential act of self-care.

> Standing in the spotlight of leadership
> is not easy and can sometimes feel like
> a curse instead of a blessing.

Kelvin A. Waites, Sr.

A leader's sphere of influence is directly tied to their success. Your sphere of influence is the people that you know, personally or professionally, in your network that care about your opinion. It is particularly important because influence is what leadership is all about.

When you are leading at a high-level, your staff and

the people closest to you know the direction you want them to go in without you even saying it. Your sphere of influence causes things to run like a well-oiled machine when you are away on vacation, out of town, or out of the country, because your people know your vision.

Your sphere of influence also has a lot to do with the culture of your organization. The people in your sphere of influence must know who you are and what you believe in because your influence can have a positive or negative effect on those around you. There are so many dynamics that go along with the impact of your influence that I believe we take it for granted daily.

Things like being authentic, having integrity, or what you entertain in terms of culture help the people in your sphere of influence to know exactly who you are. You must understand that the culture of your organization and your sphere of influence go hand in hand.

For your influence to be as effective as it can be across your sphere, it will take every leader on every level within your organization. Additionally, you will need your closest friends and family to believe in your "why" and help bring your vision to life because they are all ambassadors within your sphere of influence.

Over my 23 years in law enforcement, I have been in

the position, a couple of times, where I was new to an organization and people did not know my intentions as a new leader coming in. We all know what people do within the walls of companies and organizations when they do not have the answers. You guessed right! They fear what they do not know, and they sometimes fill in the blanks with whatever propaganda they believe that everyone else will buy into.

Hard work is universal, and it is a
language that can easily be understood
by everyone.

Kelvin A. Waites, Sr.

Joining an organization or a team at the executive level, from the outside, is no easy task. The first time that I went to a local law enforcement agency, as a part of the executive leadership team, I was viewed as an outsider. In other words, the red carpet was not exactly rolled out for me because the propaganda had already started, and my coworkers had no idea what to expect.

Everyone thought that they had it all figured out and they judged me based on what people put out there in the atmosphere. It was a challenge to win over people who had no trust or belief in me, and who just flat out did not know my intentions.

The challenge of winning people over is one of the many life experiences that has contributed to my toolbox, and I have what I consider the winning formula for those who may be suspicious or mistrustful of my intentions as a leader.

The very first thing you must do is to show up to work every single day with your sleeves rolled up. Never let anyone outwork you! You win them over by being fair and doing the right thing all the time. You win them over by not getting caught up in the gossip, rumors, or workplace cliques.

Hard work is universal, and it is a language that can easily be understood by everyone. Once your people find out that you do not mind putting in the work and you treat everyone with dignity and respect, they will gravitate towards you and your style of leadership.

Nasim Al-Hakim, CMB

Standing in the middle of the arena is one of the most peaceful places that a true leader could be in.

It is your time.

It is your backyard.

You harness it.

You take it in, soak it in, and slow it down.

You slow it down by not getting caught up in the hoopla of what is going on around you. You slow it down by being organized, prepared, and setting priorities because you understand the arena that you are standing in. You must tune out all the external factors that can make it hard for you because once again, you know, it is your time.

> Standing in the middle of the arena is one of the most peaceful places that a true leader could be in.
>
> *Nasim Al-Hakim, CMB*

I think about a quarterback in the fourth quarter of the game and it is two minutes left. Two minutes in real-time is short, right? But to a quarterback, it is a lifetime.

A quarterback will slow the game down in their head by saying, "Okay, I have 80 yards to go, so I could throw four 20-yard passes, that's going to take about 15 seconds apiece. If I make this play, then I could march down the field and put us in a position for an extra point".

You see that with the great leaders also. They can understand how to slow everything down, how to deescalate the noise, and how to be calm under pressure. The people around you will feel it as well and that is what I do when I am in the arena or on the battlefield.

I am making it mine. I do not feel the pressures of the moment because I know that I am going into it ready for whatever comes my way. I have prepared accordingly, and I understand the landscape.

A leader's sphere of influence consists of the people around them. Whether it is their family, friends, colleagues, mentors, and even adversaries, they all determine your altitude. You have heard the old saying that "birds of a feather flock together". When you are younger, you are saying to yourself, this cannot be true. I have a couple of friends who are not walking straight and narrow, but I am not like them.

As you get older, you realize when you look at groups, you see that birds of a feather flock together. There is no doubt in my mind when you look at the top

CEOs of companies, all of them are in the same circle.

Therefore, your sphere of influence will determine your altitude. Your sphere of influence can impact your progress as a leader. Your goal should be to increase the range, visibility, and strength of your sphere.

Others do not have to know your intentions as a leader if what you are doing is for the right reasons. You are the leader and if you are authentic, the people that you are called to lead will not question your intent. They will always feel safe and secure in your care.

Others do not have to know your intentions as a leader if what you are doing is for the right reasons.

Nasim Al-Hakim, CMB

My goal is not to be the most liked everywhere I go. My goal is to be someone others can look to for direction and truth. I look at coaches or those who are leading Fortune 500 companies and they are not always liked, but I think that people understand they intend to run a successful company and prosper.

You should not focus on whether they know your intentions of leading. You should focus on doing the things that you need to do personally to develop as a leader and remain consistent in who you are.

Being authentic to who you say you are is important. You do not have to walk in the room and say I am the best if they have already seen in the newspaper that you were number one. Your accomplishments will speak for themselves.

Dr. Deshawn Rouse

The stress a leader experience is real because you must show up every time and be at your best. It is like playing basketball or boxing. You do not get in the ring to train, but you get in to perform. Whenever you are showing up, you must bring your "A" game.

Therefore, you must be prepared by making time to study and focus on the task ahead of you. Also, you should get around people who can help keep you balanced, leveled, and tell you where you need to improve and what may or may not be good for you.

> This is when I realized you need to
> have a level of influence that shows
> people that you have something to say
> that they can trust and believe in.

Dr. Deshawn Rouse

The sphere of a person's influence is important. When I started as a pastor, I was just a preacher in a church. Preaching to just my people. But, over the past 21 years, because of my many works in the region, I have been recognized by national, regional, and local political leaders. As a result, my sphere of influence has changed.

People no longer see me as a novice, just saying something. Now, my words hold weight. It dawned on me one day that my influence had changed. I had some particularly important people inviting me to their events because they believed I had a certain level of influence. This is when I realized you need to have a level of influence that shows people that you have something to say and that they can trust and believe in.

People feel what you give off and if people see that you are genuine, they will trust you. If you show them love and kindness, they will begin navigating towards you.

Dr. Deshawn Rouse

If your intentions as a leader are not clear, you will have to go back to love and kindness to win people over. There is a scripture in the Bible that says, "for the lovingkindness, I have drawn thee" (Jeremiah 31:3 NIV).

People feel what you give off and if people see that you are genuine, they will trust you. If you show them love and kindness, they will begin navigating towards you. They will feel like they are valuable to you and not just a piece of property. They will also begin to perform at a different level.

CHAPTER 12

IT'S OKAY FOR YOU TO EAT TOO

Leadership nuggets covered in this chapter:

❖ Leadership is not easy.

❖ Setting aside personal hardships to lead your people.

❖ How leaders find support when they are hurting.

Kelvin A. Waites, Sr.

Leaders need to take care of themselves. If you are not taking care of yourself, your team will suffer. Your team, company, family, or organization will suffer because they will not be getting the absolute best version of you.

You must operate at a high level, physically and mentally, to move your teams and organizations to the next level. For you to work at a high level, you must be rested for the journey.

Leaders work so hard to guide, serve, and provide for our people that we must be intentional about slowing down and taking the time to take care of ourselves. If we do not, we will not be any good to anyone else.

Let me give you an example.

As leaders, when our people are hungry, it is our responsibility to go out and hunt for food. Once that leader finds the meat, they bring it back and someone must prepare it. Good leaders are used to serving so the leader takes the initiative to clean and prepare the meat to be cooked. While the food is cooking the leader sets the table for his people.

Can you guess who is responsible for serving the food once it is cooked?

You guessed right!

That is the servant leader's responsibility.

While everyone is eating, the leader watches attentively. He makes sure that everyone has everything that they need while making sure that nobody wants for anything. After some time passes, the leader realizes that he is hungry, but he has been too busy to stop and eat. Now, he goes into the kitchen to fix himself a plate, only to find that all the food is gone, and he never got a chance to get any.

By the time all of this happens, it is time for the leader to go back out and start the cycle of hunting all over again.

What leaders need to understand is that it is ok for them to eat too. If leaders do not stop for a minute to get the proper self-care, then they will destroy themselves over time and will not do anyone any good.

Therefore, if you are not getting the mental and physical rest that you should as a leader, it is going to hurt your team or organization in the long run.

You must resist the sometimes overbearing forces of your career and the workplace and continue to put your family first. At the end of the day, your career will come to an end. Either you will retire, be asked to leave, or for some unforeseen reason, you will have to leave the workplace and go home. The worst thing that can happen is that you become a stranger in your own home.

We must always remember our "why" and keep that at the forefront, no matter what. I know that it gets hard sometimes because you have so much on your plate to juggle, but you should always put your family first and embrace them as your strength. Trust me, I did not always get it.

You must be operating at a high level,
physically and mentally, to move your
teams and organizations to the next
level.

Kelvin A. Waites, Sr.

When I was a young police officer, I was a narcotics investigator for about 7 years and all I did was work. I would get off at 4:00 am or 5:00 am, go home, and find my family asleep. When they would get up to get ready for school and work, I would be asleep. Sometimes it would be two weeks at a time before we would catch up with each other and be able to sit down and talk or share a meal. At the time, it did not dawn on me that I was missing out on important moments in the lives of my family, especially my children.

It all came to a head one day when I came home from work and spoke to my daughter. As I greeted her with a hug, I called her a silly name like "hey frog head", or something like that, and she just started crying. I looked at my wife like "what's her problem?" She said, "Kelvin, I don't know where you have been for the past few months, but I told you that she started her period months ago."

At that moment in time, I felt so small and so bad. I realized that I had to do something different in terms of slowing down and spending more time with my family. My priorities were out of order and I never realized how important it was, along with my many leadership duties, to put my family first.

We all have careers and jobs, but at the end of the day, the family should come first. When our careers are over, family is all we will have left.

The silver bullet that creates an opportunity for leaders to deepen professional and personal relationships, is connecting with other people. They may not exactly look like you, talk like you, or come from the same place you come from, but, connecting with people who have absolutely nothing in common with you is a gem in itself.

I met someone years ago, during a year-long leadership class that was facilitated by the Waccamaw American Leadership Forum. The very first day of the training consisted of an orientation to the program and we were taking a ten-minute break when a friend of mine came over and said, "Hey, I want you to meet someone."

He introduced me to a lady that I had never met before. After he introduced me, he said, "Yeah I walked her over to meet you because during the break she said that you looked intimidating and angry." My friend went on to say that he told her, "You must not know Kelvin Waites. You got that one all wrong because he is a great guy." Over the next year, that young lady spent time getting to know who Kelvin Waites was.

The culmination of the training was a weeklong, outward-bound trip to the mountains of Asheville, North Carolina. A group of about 15 leaders spent a week together on a mountain without cell phones, laptops, or iPads®. It was just us, some mountain guides and a couple of people to facilitate our training. The same young lady that pre-judged me that first day at orientation said to me one day on the mountain, "Kelvin help me understand why so many African-American men are angry."

It was at that moment that I realized that when she first saw me, all she saw was an angry black man. I said, "okay" and asked her if she wanted to have this conversation. She said "absolutely" because she wanted a better understanding.

I started the conversation by saying "First and foremost, I'm not angry." She laughed and said, "I know that now Kelvin." I proceeded to explain to her that throughout history, some things have happened and the world that she came from may look different than mine. We talked about everything from slavery to racism, white privilege, unfair practices in the workplace, and diversity, over about an hour and a half. Even though it was a great conversation the young lady was almost in tears by the end of it, because she realized that what she saw as anger in black men was really in most cases, pain, and frustration.

Both of us had a breakthrough that day. We connected and are the best of friends today because

---

The silver bullet that creates an opportunity for leaders to deepen professional and personal relationships, is connecting with other people.

Kelvin A. Waites, Sr.

she had enough courage to ask some tough questions. She had a burning desire to get a better understanding of who I was. I realized that we cannot always hold everyone accountable for what they do not know, and sometimes especially when the opportunity presents itself, we must take the initiative to educate them.

As I see it, connecting with people is the silver bullet that allows leaders to not only deepen but strengthen professional and personal relationships.

Nasim Al-Hakim, CMB

For a long time, I have said a somewhat contradictory phrase, "I am selfishly unselfish. I am not sure where it came from and I know it may not make sense to some of you but stay with me as I explain its meaning.

I am selfish because I must focus on achieving what I know I must get from point A to point B. There will be a time in this process when I may have to tune some things out. I will have to choose not to deal with certain things because I must remain focused on the path that is taking me to point B. Then when I get to point B, I will have the ability to lean back and pull others up to point B with me and that is the unselfish part.

I think a lot of leaders feel like you should move at the same pace and at the same time as the people around you but unfortunately, that is not true. There will be times when there is going to be a lot of blue water between you and others, but you can assist them and help them pick up the pace. This is done in front of the pack, hence the blue water between you sets the tone for the journey.

It is extremely hard to balance your career and your family life. At any given time either will feel like they are being compromised. That is going to happen. The goal for me is to have that aligned within my lifestyle.

My family knows what I am called to do and shares in my path as I do with them. The President of the United States, a coach of a professional sports team, and a reporter all work long hours and spend minimal time with their families. It is a conversation and a sacrifice all in one for all parties.

It is extremely hard to balance your
career and your family life. At any
given time either will feel like they are
being compromised.

Nasim Al-Hakim, CMB

However, it goes back to vision. My family and I have a shared vision of success and we follow the plan. As leaders, we should share our professional vision along with creating a family vision, so all members know what is ahead. That is the secret sauce to spending quality time when you can.

In my eyes, communication is the way to deepen professional and personal relationships. We all talk about it all the time in our relationships and at work. We must communicate, but many times we leave out the second part, connection. We fail to make the connection.

The silver bullet is connectivity and here is an

example of the difference between communication and connecting.

If you turn on the light switch, you are communicating. But when you have electricity, that allows for connectivity so the switch can communicate with the light source and you can have light in the room.

We must communicate, but many times
we leave out the second part,
connection.

Nasim Al-Hakim, CMB

This is true in relationships as well. You cannot stop at communication and expect to know what you need to know to be successful. You must deepen your relationships by asking open-ended questions, that allow you to learn more than just what is on the surface.

Spend time and be sincere. Taking the time to do these simple things will increase your connectivity and deepen your rapport with everyone.

Dr. Deshawn Rouse

According to Webster, the definition of self-care is caring for oneself. I keep relating a lot to the Bible and what was said in the book of Genesis. The Bible says that on the seventh day God rests. I believe it is especially important that all leaders take time for self-care. And when I say that it goes back to some of the things I said earlier. I am talking about exercise or even taking time to go get a massage, pedicure, manicure, and haircut/hairdo.

> A lot of leaders carry stress and pressure and they need to learn to unwind so that they can be more effective.
>
> *Dr. Deshawn Rouse*

All those things make you feel better about yourself and I believe that when you do that for yourself, you feel better when you get around people. People will feel better because you give off that feeling. And so, I believe in any organization, our team is going to be successful.

A lot of leaders carry stress and pressure and they need to learn to unwind so that they can be more effective.

As it pertains to leaders, resisting the forces that can place your families second. You must remember that you can get so driven on the success that you start to lose focus on who is important. The most important people in your life are your family, your wife, husband, children, parents, and you must always keep these relationships intact. The worst thing you can do is arrive at your destination and nobody is there to celebrate with you. I believe that family needs to be on board so they can enjoy the journey with you. So many times, they cannot relate because they know nothing of it.

I believe it is important for them to see your journey and know what you are doing. If they can see how you did it, especially your children, they will be able to do the same thing or possibly take over a family business.

They also need to see you be human and a businessperson at the same time. You must have a leisure time with those who are important. The kids must enjoy you as you excel, and they grow up. Your spouse must feel like they are apart and not just sitting on the sidelines watching.

We must be open to other people's perspectives. We live on the planet Earth and it has 7.5 billion people on it. That is a lot of different thinking patterns. I think we should be open to other people's perspectives around us. We should be able to hear what other people say about an issue. When we do that, we can get involved in new orbits. I do not believe you can go to the top without using other people's orbits to send you there.

When you try to get there yourself, you just bring all your rocket fuel and you will not get far.

What do I mean?

When satellites launch in space, they use orbits to the earth and as the satellite goes out, they use other planets' orbits to spin the satellites to other orbits.

Having different people's perspectives around you helps propel you to places you could not easily get into. Even though you may feel you don't have anything to say to a surgeon because you are a minister, still say it because if that's your profession, you should still have something in you to take them to another level.

> Having different people's perspectives
> around you, it helps propel you to
> places you could not easily get into.
>
> *Dr. Deshawn Rouse*

Likewise, listen to the surgeon even though you think they do not have anything to tell you. They could take you to another level. They may introduce you to someone that can help usher you into another area. Remember, everyone has something unique to bring to the table.

I love Jesus and how He picked several people to be on His team. He had financial realm people, contractors, and fishermen. These guys were all businessmen. Imagine that, the all-knowing son of God had different people's perspectives walking with Him. He intended for it to be that way to show us no matter how smart you think you may be; you still need someone else to help you along the way.

He told his disciples, "I'm going to make you fishermen of men." Isn't it amazing He used their profession to relate to them on a greater scale?

CHAPTER 13

LEAD WHILE YOU BLEED

Leadership nuggets covered in this chapter:

❖ Leading others is not easy.

❖ How to set aside personal hardships and led your people.

❖ When leaders are hurt, they need support too.

Kelvin A. Waites, Sr.

Leading people is not an easy thing to do! If it was easy, then no one would need help to figure it out, and writing this book would not be a good business decision.

Leading people is extremely hard because oftentimes you end up carrying your load, plus the load of the people that you are called to lead. Daily, you will make decisions that impact people's lives, and everyone will not be happy. The term "the road of leadership is very narrow" is a true statement. As you get promoted and progress along the way in your leadership journey, you will sometimes lose friends because everyone cannot go where you need to go for you to be successful. You will also need to make sacrifices along the way because you must put your people first.

It goes back to what I talked about in a previous chapter. Leaders must have balance when it comes to their mind, body, and soul because the impact of leadership has the potential to shake you to your very core. Leading people can be extremely rewarding, but it can be very grueling and brutal as well.

If a leader is going to put their personal stuff and hardships aside and lead their people, they must first recognize that they are equipped with everything that they need to get the job done. I often say to people that "when God washes your car, he doesn't just wash the trunk and the hood. He washes the entire car and details the inside". In other words, he gives us everything that we need for the journey.

If a leader is going to put their personal stuff and hardships aside and lead your people, they must first recognize that they are equipped with everything that they need to get the job done.

Kelvin A. Waites, Sr.

When I attended a conference several years ago at Bishop TD Jakes' church in Texas, the theme of the conference was "lead while you bleed." Attending the conference was not something that I had planned, but I was glad that I attended it because it completely changed my life. I was invited by a pastor from a local church, who I met at a weekly Bible study breakfast for men.

One day he approached me and said, "Do you want to go to a training conference in Dallas?" I asked, "What kind of training?", and his response was "leadership training". Unbeknownst to him, I was a Dallas Cowboys fan and all I could think about was having a chance to see the Dallas Cowboys stadium (also known as Jerry's World).

I was reluctant and I knew my decision to go would not be based on attending the conference or training at all. But my wife said, "Hey you need to go because you never take any time off." So, with that, I decided to go, and over the week, I heard some very dynamic speakers.

The funny thing was that I could not understand and figure out why I was there. I went with a group of three pastors, even though I was just a Lieutenant at the local Sheriff's Office. Initially, I questioned why I was even invited. In the end, I figured out that God arranged for me to be there. That experience helped me to understand that as a leader, I am human, and I can get emotionally scratched and beat up.

That conference reminded me that I also have ups and downs like everyone else, but at the end of the day, I still must lead my people. They do not want to hear that the Chief cannot lead them today because he has a headache or because his kids acted out last night and he just does not feel like leading. They need direction, they need your vision, and most importantly they need your leadership. We need to put our hardships, pain, and frustration from our personal lives aside, and lead our people because we were created and wired the way we are for that purpose. Leaders have that extra "thing" that allows us to carry our weight, as well as the weight of the people that we are called to lead.

That conference taught me and gave me the confidence to realize that I was built to "lead while I bleed" just like many of you are. There is a great responsibility that comes along with our pay raises, company cars, fringe benefits, as well as our corner offices with the window. "To whom much is given, much is required."

It is extremely important for leaders of strong faith

It is critical that leaders get the
support, assistance and treatment
needed for them to lead at a high level.

Kelvin A. Waites, Sr.

to acknowledge that God put us where we are for a reason and a season. We must realize that He will never fail us as we continue to climb the ladder of leadership. As you continue to climb, your circle will get smaller and smaller and you will be forced to rely on your faith, destiny, or whatever it is you believe in. In addition to relying on your faith, be sure to lean on your family when things get tough because they will always be there for you. Make sure not to alienate yourself from them along the way.

Leaders also need to have a mentor or close friend that we can lean on when times get hard or we are hurting. When all else fails and none of the above works or is available to you, seek counseling. A lot of times leaders are reluctant to ask for help because they believe that it is a sign of weakness. It's also hard for leaders to open up and trust people with certain pieces of delicate information because, a lot of times, people have their agendas that are not in the best interest of you as an individual and your team or organization.

Most companies and organizations have employee assistance programs (EAP) to assist employees with hardships. Leaders should take full advantage of this resource and know that when we break, we cannot automatically fix ourselves. Leaders must get the support, assistance, and treatment needed for them to lead at a high level. The bottom line is that "people who are hurting, hurt other people." Seek the help that you need or else you will not be any good to or for anybody else.

Nasim Al-Hakim, CMB

I am going to start by saying it is not an easy thing to do if you do not know how to lead yourself. For me, that is simple. You lead yourself. You lead your process. You lead your people, right? I think that it starts with yourself. If you are not organized, if you do not have a foundation in leadership, you do not have something that works, then it is going to be hard to lead people. I use sports analogies a lot because I think that it is universal.

Leadership is not about an emotional journey. It is about an honest journey, a true journey. You know the old saying "you take the good with the bad, take the bitter with the sweet", that's leadership. Everything does not always come about the way you wanted it to and you can have some feelings about it.

> Leadership is not about an emotional journey. It is about an honest journey, a true journey.

Nasim Al-Hakim, CMB

Our hardships or other personal challenges have nothing to do with the task on hand. That is what it means to lead while you bleed. If I have a death in my family, I go to work, and I am dealing with it. I have people who are depending on me to lead them to where we must go. Yes, I am human and yes, it hurts but, once I get out there, I do what I must do and push past the emotions. I must deliver, and I must be accountable for what I need to be accountable for.

For leaders, once again, that is internal, and we must deal with that. And we can't come back and put it on anyone else or we can come back in and make others' lives harder because we don't know how to deal with what we have in front of us personally. We can also trust and share with our people, so they know what we are facing and have mutual support. This increases a more inclusive and family environment.

Family members, your sphere of influence, and friends are the people leaders should look to for support. If you are religious, whatever denomination, you should also turn to your faith. For me, my family is the first place I turn to for support.

I have a niece who's 6 years old and she has been through something tragic. She was severely burned. She had second and third-degree burns to her face from hot grease and I was devastated. Just talking about it right now, hurts me to my core. She was only four and she was in a coma for three weeks. She finally came out of it and had surgery to put her face back to normalcy. It was burnt to a crisp and I was deflated for almost a year. She has since recovered and is back to being a kid again.

I had a conversation with my sister once, and she told me an eye-opening story. She told me that she went to school with her one day and the kids were so happy to see her back at school. The kids looked at her and said, 'Hey what happened to your face?" And she said "Well, I was burned". Then two of the little kids told her "It's going to be okay. It's only a rash, it'll go away".

This story reminds me that kids do not see what we

> So, when you have one of those rough days, just find something to do that is going to bring you comfort.

Nasim Al-Hakim, CMB

as adults internalize. Whenever I need support, I turn to my niece because she simplifies everything for me. You know, I jokingly say "Hey I had a rough day today". She will reply, "Well, you can just play with your toys". That makes me laugh because in her world after those days and bad times... just playing with your toys makes everything okay.

I also find myself calling my niece whenever I need a little pep talk as well. I will call her, sit back, and listen to her share simple tips for living. She slows life down for me and keeps me grounded by the way she simply talks without trying to solve my problem or my challenge. She is showing me how to be happy and I am thankful for that in her.

So, when you have one of those rough days, just find something to do that is going to bring you comfort. Everything will be okay. It is that simple.

Dr. Deshawn Rouse

Leading can be easy and hard. When we speak about something being easy, it is usually with the mindset of no problems attached and that is not the way life goes. If you are doing anything worthwhile, challenges will come with it. One of the challenges is dealing with people with different personalities.

You must pray and ask God to show you how to deal with your people. In the Bible, there is a scripture of King Solomon asking God to show him how to deal with His people. And the Bible said God answered by giving King Solomon wisdom (II Chronicles 1:7-12). Leading people can be challenging, but with God's grace, He will show you how to effectively lead them. It is when leaders do it on their own that challenges will arise.

> If you are doing anything worthwhile,
> challenges will come with it.

Dr. Deshawn Rouse

Let me share a personal story with you. In May of 2019, my wife was diagnosed with cancer. Being a pastor with pastoral duties, a real estate investor, and working in finance with the stock market, I had teams that were depending on me to show up. I had to do my duties and handle business. I would have lost a lot of business deals or my members may have lost focus if I would have given in to my emotions and stopped leading. We as leaders can never let our emotions get the best of us.

Many of my people knew nothing of what was going on because I made sure to exude strength. I had to learn to lead while I bleed. This reminds me of a shepherd who set out to find himself having to free wayward sheep that walk-off from the fold. Those sheep get entangled in briers and the shepherd will take his bare hands and pull the briers off the sheep. The sheep runs away free, but because of the briers on the shepherd's bare hands, he is now bleeding. That same shepherd goes back to tending his sheep even though he is bleeding.

The number one person the leader should look to is God. He is the only one that can understand them better than anyone else.

Dr. Deshawn Rouse

Sometimes leaders wish they could let everyone see them cry as I said in a previous chapter. But the reality is, unless the people know what it is like to lead, they will never understand the cry. Cry in your room, dry your face, and report for duty. It goes back earlier to what I said in the book. You must be tenacious. You must learn to take a hit like a football player and report back to the huddle to learn the next play.

The number one person the leader should look to is God. He is the only one that can understand them better than anyone else. God made us social beings, so we should have mentors that we could confide in when we are hurting. We should be able to say to them "I am weak, I need help, and I need advice". The person that you go to should be someone you can trust, someone who is not waiting to see your downfall but can put something back into you. They should be someone that when you are not feeling well and mentally drained, they can pray for you and give you wisdom through their life experiences.

CHAPTER 14

CAN'T AFFORD TO HAVE A BAD DAY

Leadership nuggets covered in this chapter:

❖ There are no "bad" days for leaders.

❖ The difference between sight and vision.

❖ Never lose sight of your leadership responsibility.

Kelvin A. Waites, Sr.

As leaders, tone-setters, change agents, and game-changers we cannot afford to have bad days because there is too much at stake. Whether you woke up with a headache today, you and your spouse are not getting along, your kids are acting out, or maybe your neighbor's dog barked all night, you still cannot afford to have a bad day.

Before you get angry, close this book, and throw it in the corner, hear me out.

> Our vision is that thing that lives within the future and is what leaders need to help everyone around them work and move forward.
>
> *Kelvin A. Waites, Sr.*

I know we are human and, technically, we do have bad days as leaders, but we cannot let our people see it. Suppose one of your people came to see you because they were having serious issues with something, only to find you in a foul mood. Do you think that your employee would want to complicate your day even more or make it worse? I am going to put myself out on a limb and say no. Furthermore, just that quick you missed out on an opportunity to lead.

Now, I did not always think this way, but something happened during my career that changed my entire outlook and perspective on leadership.

Several years ago, early one Sunday afternoon, one of my employees called me and when I answered the phone they said, "Hey I hate to bother you." My response was "You are no bother at all. How can I help you?" My employee went on to tell me that they had a profoundly serious issue that they were trying to deal with on their own but realized that they needed help. Fortunately, at the time, the organization that I worked for had an exceptional employee assistance program. We were able to get the employee the assistance that they needed to get better.

Months later, the employee returned to work, and everything was good. Months after that, I received another call from that same employee one afternoon. When I saw who was calling me, I automatically thought to myself "Oh hell, this can't be good." I automatically thought the worst, but the employee was calling to thank me for what I had previously done.

I humbly told the employee that no thanks was needed because I just did my job and followed policy. The employee said, "Nah you don't understand because you did more than just your job that day." The employee proceeded to tell me that on the day of the first call they were prepared to take their life and that if I had not answered the phone, they would have gone through with it. They also said had I not given them the answers that they needed in terms of getting the help that they needed, they would have taken their life. According to the employee, the weapon was in their hand while they were speaking to me on the phone.

I was in shock and total disbelief. Finally, my employee told me that the only reason that they even bothered to call me was that I NEVER SEEMED TO HAVE A BAD DAY! To them, I was always approachable and always willing to listen. This experience changed me forever and helped me to see leadership on a different level.

Even though we may be going through stuff, we must put our stuff aside. Even though we may be scratched and beat up emotionally, we must put the best out front for them to see. In my case, leadership was a matter of life or death. It could be a different situation for you, but whatever it is, as leaders we cannot afford to have bad days.

There are so many intangibles that go along with leadership. So many that I cannot list them all. There are so many twists, turns, peaks, and valleys to this leadership journey and leaders need to understand the difference between sight and vision. Sight is what we see right in front of us out on the horizon. It is what we can touch, smell, see and taste right now. In terms of leadership, you can call sight your awareness of everything around you.

Sight is the essence of our presence. The dictionary defines sight as "the power or faculty of seeing; perception of objects by use of the eyes." Our vision is that thing that lives within the future and is what leaders need to help everyone around them work and move towards.

The funny thing is that vision likens to faith because

Sight satisfies our now, but our vision
gives us hope for the future.

Kelvin A. Waites, Sr.

it requires us to believe in things that we cannot see, initially. We will have obstacles within our sight, but it is our job as leaders to help our people see beyond their now. You want them to focus on the horizon, while hoping, believing, and searching to see the vision. The dictionary defines vision as "the act or power of anticipating that which will or may come to be."

Sight satisfies our now, but our vision gives us hope for the future. That is the difference between sight and vision, and it is up to the leader to make sure that their people continue to have hope to be able to work towards the vision.

We can never lose sight of our responsibility to lead our people because our people are our greatest resource. Leaders need to acknowledge and recognize that we do not get it done by ourselves. Without the support, collaboration, and cooperation of my staff there is no way that I can be successful.

Any good leader will tell you that their staffs are the real heroes that make it happen day in and day out. It is all about the team. When leaders lose sight of that and act as if they got it going on, got it all figured out and they do not need their teams, that is when their effectiveness as a leader will decline. We must have compassion for our people and remember to build them up instead of tearing them down.

Oftentimes, as leaders, we are under tremendous stress and we lash out at the people who are closest to us. We can never lose sight of our responsibility to lead our people because without them we are nothing. I know it is a hard pill to swallow but it is true. Whether we believe it or not, or even admit it, we need our people just as bad, if not more, than they need us.

Nasim Al-Hakim, CMB

We cannot afford to have bad days as people, because we do not know when the day is going to come when we are no longer here. This concept does not just apply to leaders. We as people often complain about things we cannot control; we take on the burdens of the world. This happens because we are trying to do things that are out of our span and it consumes us.

> The difference between sight and vison
> is that sight can be seen and vision, the
> unseen, is created.

Nasim Al-Hakim, CMB

As a leader, you cannot have a bad day because you set the tone for your group or your team. When you walk into the office and you smile in the morning, everybody feels happy. If you walk into the office upset and slam your door, you set the tone for people to walk on eggshells. If you are driving for results, you will not reach those results by being negative. It does not work that way unless you are looking for negative results.

Leaders and people alike cannot afford to have a bad day because this day that we are talking about could truly be your last.

The difference between sight and vision is that sight can be seen and vision, the unseen, is created. I believe the difference between the two is that vision can include sight, but it goes a step further and in terms of leadership, successful leaders are visionaries.

We must never lose sight of our responsibilities as a leader and our obligation to those we are called to lead.

Nasim Al-Hakim, CMB

As a leader, you are not the leader that you may think you are. In cases of leadership, one typically says when somebody is in charge, the other person is submissive or subservient. But think about it. What they are saying is, "I am going to allow you to manage or assist me with this process to the point where I need to get to help". You must handle them with care. We must never lose sight of our responsibilities as a leader and our obligation to those we are called to lead.

Dr. Deshawn Rouse

You should never let a bad day overtake you. Leaders need to stay consistent. We live in a society where we depend on people showing up and giving us their best on their bad days.

For example, take your lawyers, doctors, firemen, and policemen. We expect these people to show up with their "A" game, no matter what their personal lives hold. When you are a leader, you must put your bad day in the background and perform for the people you are assigned to. If your bad day causes you to have an attitude, you can cause people to get in their emotions and not perform at their optimal level.

A leader must learn to master their
emotions. I am not saying do not cry
but learn where to cry.

Dr. Deshawn Rouse

Like I stated in the last chapter, my wife was diagnosed with cancer, and many days, I was under a lot of emotional pressure. But, when it was time for me to go before God's people, I had to encourage myself. If I had gone into the service talking negatively and saying things contrary to my faith, then the very people I was supposed to be helping deepen their faith in God could lose their faith because of my actions.

A leader must learn to master their emotions. I am not saying do not cry but learn where to cry. Remember that people are depending on you. They may not understand what you are going through, but if you have been called to lead, that is what they are looking for, your leadership.

The difference between sight and vision is that sight is mainly what you see. Vision deals with what you do not see outwardly, but what you see inwardly. There is a scripture in the Bible that says, "We walk by faith and not by sight." Every leader should be a visionary. You must be able to operate outside of limitations, and sight produces limitations.

Vision breaks boundaries. You must be able to look at a piece of property everyone else sees as junk and see what the future of it can be. That is a true leader. The leader must be able to take people who can just see the sight and show them what it is going to be and how we are going to get there.

I believe it is important that you never lose sight because it is not about you. It is about the people you are serving. It is never about what you can get out of the people. It is about getting people to better their lives.

It is never about what you can get out
of the people. It is about getting the
people to better their lives.

Dr. Deshawn Rouse

In church, the word "minister" means servant. I must keep in mind that I am here to serve people. I am not a king. Keeping in mind that service is my responsibility, is what allows me to see lives get better. In return for that service, people will celebrate you and give you accolades. If the greatest leader, Jesus washed people's feet, then I can serve people as well. Remember the lowest position can be the highest position of all.

ABOUT THE AUTHORS

Kelvin A. Waites, Sr.

www.kelvinwaites.com
Facebook.com/kelvin.waites.5
Instagram.com/kelvin.waites.5
Twitter.com/waiteskelvin
Linkedin.com/in/kelvin-waites-220a7624

Veteran, chief, dad, husband, mentor, coach, author, founder, and leader are all words used by people that follow the leadership of Kelvin Waites. As a person committed to building strong leaders, Chief Kelvin received a Bachelor of Science Degree from Charleston Southern University in Organizational Management, a Professional Coaching Certification from Atiras International, authored, "Hit'em Before They Hit You", and launched Waites Lifted LLC. (a private leadership and life coaching practice). Coach Kelvin is also a graduate of the prestigious F.B.I. National Academy (class #248) and the DEA's Drug Unit Commander's Academy (class # 60). Both are located in Quantico Virginia.

Chief Kelvin began his law enforcement career in 1997 after serving as a member of the United States Army in the field of military Intelligence. Having led more than ten thousand individuals over the past twenty years, it's fair to say, Coach Kelvin is an experienced and well-equipped leader. Accolades, honors, and awards have been named in his honor, yet Chief Kelvin remains humble while focusing on building stronger communities one leader, conversation, and example at a time.

His impeccable record and accomplishments have positioned him to be a highly sought-after speaker, presenter, and coach. His emphasis is always on leading, growing, and reaching. His strong faith inspires the masses to pursue excellence, even when excellence requires a huge stretch. He stands on his life's motto, "We are all actors in God's production". The inclusion of all mankind pushes him to pursue success beyond applause, awards, and ovations.

Chief Kelvin currently serves as a Chief of Police, the Board Chair for AMI Kids of Georgetown, member of the board of Directors for the Salvation Army for Georgetown & Williamsburg Counties, a board member for The Village Group, as well as a committee member on the Human Rights Committee for the Georgetown Department of Disabilities & Special needs. Chief Waites is also a member of Alpha Phi Alpha Fraternity, Incorporated. He enjoys connecting with young people and helping his community. His favorite saying is "Don't just be good, be good for something."

Nasim Al-Hakim, CMB

www.nasimalhakim.com
Facebook.com/nasim.alhakim.12
Instagram.com/nasdaqnas718
Twitter.com/NasimAlHakim1
Linkedin.com/in/nasim-al-hakim-cmb®-5a7b9b5

Born in Brooklyn, NY, Nasim Al-Hakim, CMB is no stranger to the power of wise decisions and commitment to excellence. He dedicates his strong work ethic to his native Trinidadian mother who sacrificed and worked multiple jobs to provide for him and his sister. Before his senior year of high school, Nasim and his family moved from the bustling streets of city life to Columbia, SC, and this is where he uncovered his potential for a future that had not existed before. Through a sheer determination to succeed, Nasim was able to graduate from high school, work several jobs to put himself through college, and earn his

Bachelor of Arts in Government and International Politics from George Mason University.

From there, the path Nasim chose brought him to Capitol Hill where he worked amongst Washington's elite minds and politicians. Consequently, Nasim was chosen to work in legislative positions within the U.S. House of Representatives and the U.S. Senate. Since then, he has cultivated a vast portfolio of servant leadership roles, ranging from mentoring students in the inner city to several management roles in mortgage banking. Nasim is on a mission to guide and assist leaders in helping families build financial wealth through avenues like education, training, advocacy, and leadership. Self-trained as a mortgage broker, Nasim began his lending career in 2004. Primarily serving in the Southeast region of the United States, Nasim has extensive experience in all channels of origination including retail, wholesale, correspondent, and direct-to-consumer.

Nasim has led successful mortgage teams intending to raise others to be effective leaders who motivate individuals to work together to achieve a common goal. He has served on several boards for trade associations and non-profit organizations. His willingness to give back and pay it forward is significant in the communities that he serves. With the motto, "You can only control what you can control...your past does not dictate the trajectory of your future," Nasim seeks to not only continue to lead professionally but to enrich the lives of those who work alongside him.

In 2019, Nasim obtained the highest certification in the mortgage industry, Certified Mortgage Banker. This prestigious designation symbolizes respect, credibility, ethics, and achievement within the real estate finance industry. Having earned the CMB designation, Nasim is among an elite group of professionals at the top of their trade who have achieved the highest level of professional success.

Currently, Nasim resides in Charlotte, NC where he is focused on his professional development and running a successful company. As the founder of the Wise Advisory Group, LLC, he is grooming other industry leaders in hopes of helping individuals and families gain their legacies of leadership and wealth.

Dr. Deshawn Rouse

www.deshawnrouse.com
Facebook.com/deshawn.rouse.9
Instagram.com/drouse0556
Twitter.com/DeshawnRouse2
Linkedin.com/in/deshawn-rouse

Dr. Deshawn Rouse, founder/chief executive officer of Spirit-Filled Ambassadors for Christ Ministries was founded in 1999. He serves as Senior Pastor and the Senior Prelate of the United Ministries of the Kingdom, which was founded in 2013. Dr. Rouse is a progressive visionary who loves humanity and sees it at its best. He has been serving his community for the past 25 years. This movement was founded in 1999, and under his dynamic and quintessential leadership, the church's humble inception became with no members. Four short years later in November 2003, construction began on a half-million-dollar edifice. In 2005, he led his young congregation to purchase a 16-passenger van and to also purchase a 6,000 square-foot building. This building is known as the Executive Center (a multi-purpose building), which is the East Campus for the ministry, that sits facing the main edifice. In 2008, a 28-passenger transportation bus and a 16-passenger van were purchased. In 2013, a 57-passenger Charter bus was purchased. In May 2019, a 59-passenger charter bus was purchased

Born to Jacob and Ellen Rouse, Dr. Deshawn Rouse is the youngest of his siblings. Dr. Rouse received his calling into ministry in the year 1997 and was ordained as an Elder in the Lord's Church in the year 1999. Dr. Rouse received his Doctoral Degree in Biblical Studies in the year of 2013 from North Carolina College of Theology in Wilmington, North Carolina.

Dr. Deshawn Rouse is also the founder of many events that are brought to the community every year, that purpose entertainment and betterment of people. One of the highlighted events is "Spirit Fest", which is in its 20th year and has served thousands over the past two decades. This event encompasses carnival rides, helicopter rides, game trucks, free food for everyone, a car show, a fireworks show, an outdoor Gospel concert, and many other activities. There is also a bi-annual circus event that is brought to the town which has entertained many within the Afro-Americans, Caucasian, Hispanic, Indian, and African American communities. Dr. Rouse is also the founder of an annual Christmas giveaway event for the underprivileged within the community. He is also the founder of an annual clean-up, "Beautification Project", which includes cleaning up and renovating around the Andrews City Hall, Police Department, Fire Department, Magistrate Office, the Library, and other governmental buildings for the beautification of the city.

Dr. Deshawn Rouse has served on various boards that include

the Planning Commission for the municipality of Andrews, South Carolina where he served as vice-chairman from 2013-2017, the Zoning Board of Appeals for the municipality of Andrews, South Carolina from 2017 where he serves as a board member. He serves as the vice-chairman of Smurfs Developmental School from 2011 to currently. He is a covenant partner with Helping Hands of Georgetown from 2017 to current. Dr. Rouse is also the founder/chief executive officer of a state and federal prison ministry, called the Prison of Hope Ministry, where ministry is done monthly with prayer and words of encouragement. The Prison of Hope Ministry encompasses Lieber, Turbeville, Evans, Broad River, Goodman Correction Institute, and Georgetown & Kingstree Detention Centers.

After hearing about his outstanding work in the community, the head coach of the NFL team, the Carolina Panthers autographed and gave him a citizen's award. Dr. Deshawn Rouse has received numerous awards for his distinguished work in the community by local and national leaders, some include the Andrews South Carolina Chapter of the NAACP. An Icon Award was given in 2018. He also received the Town of Andrews Citizens Award from 2016-2019 from the Honorable Mayor Frank McClary, and the South Carolina State House of Representatives, Representative Carl L. Anderson in 2014. In 2014, he also received several commendations, and a motion was made by the South Carolina General Assembly House of Representative for honor and recognition, and from the South Carolina Lieutenant Governor, J. Yancey McGill, for a Leadership and Dedication Award. Another award was given by the Governor's Office of South Carolina, Nikki Haley, who is the former Ambassador to the United Nations for the United States of America in 2016. In 2016, United States Senator, Tim Scott, Junior United States

Senator from South Carolina gave him a prominent award. In the year 2017, the United States House of Representatives gave him two awards, one from the democratic party, James Clyburn (6th Congressional District), and one from the republican party, Tom Rice (7th Congressional District). In 2017, Governor Henry McMaster of the State of South Carolina gave him an award.

Dr. Rouse is known as a humble man that never brings attention to himself. He believes that you cannot love God, and not love on the people that you encounter each day. Therefore, he is not biased and gives everyone a chance. Dr. Rouse is married to the beautiful and supportive Lady Debra Rouse. They have three handsome sons, Tarique Scott, Kenly, and Jordan Rouse, whom he cherishes with all of his heart.